When We Were Young in Africa

Carol Claxon Polsgrove

OTHER BOOKS BY CAROL POLSGROVE

Ending British Rule in Africa: Writers in a Common Cause

Divided Minds: Intellectuals and the Civil Rights Movement

*It Wasn't Pretty, Folks, But Didn't We
Have Fun? Esquire in the Sixties*

When We Were Young in Africa
1948-1960

by Carol Claxon Polsgrove

Culicidae Press

Culicidae Press, LLC
918 5th Street
Ames, IA 50010
USA
www.culicidaepress.com

editor@culicidaepress.com

Culicidae
PRESS, LLC
culicidaepress.com

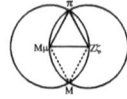

Ames | Gainesville | Lemgo | Rome

For more information, please visit www.culicidaepress.com

ISBN: 978-1-941892-07-7

Cover design and interior layout © 2015 by polytekton.com
Author photo by Carol Stangler

For Cora

West Africa in 1940, eight years before we sailed for the Gold Coast
(Wikipedia Commons)

Contents

Imagine you are watching a movie and suddenly the action stops and the credits begin to roll. Leaving Africa was like that. I had been going along in my African story, full of its sights and sounds and smells—children balancing kerosene tins on their heads, drums rumbling at night, air scented by smoke from charcoal and wood fires. . . And then: Cut. It was over.

After twelve years of growing up mostly in West Africa, I was back in the United States, where people thought growing up in Africa was strange and growing up the daughter of missionaries was even stranger. I learned to avoid mentioning that part of my life at all, because if I did, I would feel the stereotypes close round me. I did my best to pass as American without ever quite succeeding. When my mother asked me in her last days, "Do you appreciate your African childhood?" I replied with cruel honesty, "Yes, but now I don't belong in America."

Just weeks after her death at the age of ninety-six, I sat myself down in a state of survivor's freedom to explore the childhood I had tried to put behind me. I poured out memories across a yellow notepad and began reading the letters Mother had passed on to me—intimate letters she and Daddy had written back to family in Kentucky, letters I myself had written from my boarding school in Nigeria. As a historian I already understood the richness of life told in letters: the way secrets spring from their pages. Thus innocently (if any historian can be said to be innocent) I began—and found myself tangled up in a story I had not just forgotten but had never known.

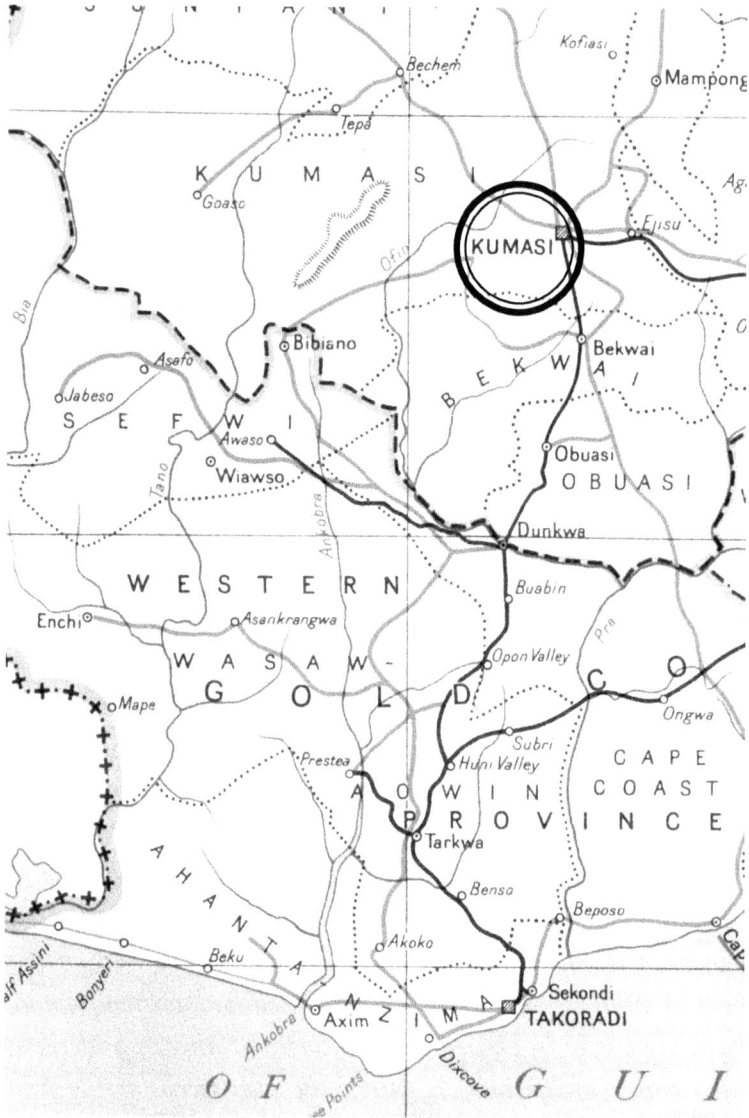

Gold Coast, 1948

(*Modified detail of a map published by the Directorate of Colonial*
Surveys and printed by the War Office of the United Kingdom)

That Is What the Matter Is

Hardly any travellers now realize what I learned at the age of three: how vast is the expanse of water that separates the world's continents. My daughter and her friends have flown from one continent to another. None has yet taken a ship from the United States to Europe, much less from the United States to Africa—days on the blue sea with its distant horizon and the ship itself nearly always alone.

I can scare myself now just thinking about that little ship by itself on the great Atlantic and little me on that little ship, though at the time, to judge from the letters Mother and Daddy wrote home, I did not seem worried at all. I was the only child on board; everyone watched over me. Mother made a harness for me so I would not fall overboard. The first mate hung up a swing for me. The chief engineer gave me a doll. The chief steward gave me cookies and fruit. The nurse gave me candy. Daddy made a hypodermic needle out of modeling clay and I—remembering all the shots we'd had before we started out—gave him a shot.

While Mother suffered seasickness for the first few days on board and Daddy thought about storms that would send us to our deaths were it not for God watching over us, the only thing that bothered me was the loud blast of the foghorn at a distant ship our first night. I remember the foghorn, and I remember the little dog on the ship that jumped into the sea and how the first mate stopped the ship so we could all look for the dog in the great sea of choppy water and how someone saw him and a sailor jumped in and brought him back to the ship and put him into a bucket lowered down from the deck and climbed up a rope ladder himself to safety.

And I remember the very day I came to shore in the Gold Coast.

The ship had docked outside the port of Takoradi, where there was no room for us yet in the harbor. My parents went ashore on a launch to go through customs, leaving me behind with a fellow passenger for what they thought would be a few hours. When the captain discovered they were gone, he was furious. It would be the next day or longer before the ship could get into port and the sea had turned too rough for Mother and Daddy to get back to the ship.

And so he himself carried me down a swaying gangplank and with a great leap landed us both in a little boat rising and falling with each swell of the wave. I remember the leap, the little boat rising up and down on the dark water below us, how the captain jumped and nearly fell—but how safe I was in his arms.

✗◦

From Takoradi, the Gold Coast port where we landed on June 9, 1948, we rode a train through a deep forest, accompanied by the Yoruba pastor of the Baptist church in Kumasi, our destination. In the three years of my life in segregated Kentucky, I had possibly never met a black person, though surely I had seen black people in Louisville, where we'd lived at the Southern Baptist seminary. Now, everyone around us was black, even our fellow Baptists who met us at the train station in Kumasi, and I wanted to know why, and when Mother said God made them that way, I wanted to know why he made so many.

We saw no other white person the next day when we walked to church among the crowds—barbers plying their trade, women wearing colorful headties and babies on their backs. At the Baptist Church, started by Yorubas from Nigeria, we were the only white people there, too, except for the albino man who walked around with a stick taking whacks at noisy children. I remember him well, how he looked like me, but not—his fuzzy hair murky yellow. He frightened me, and so did the big mean-looking vultures perched on the walls around the courtyard where we sat, their long necks raw pink, their bulging eyes peering down at the crowd looking for prey, ready to pounce, especially on the one small blonde girl wearing glasses—me.

We went to church twice that day, once in the morning and again in the afternoon. Daddy prayed for the dedication of two babies and in the afternoon service, preached. An interpreter from Nigeria translated his English words into Yoruba, sentence by sentence. "This has been a great day," Daddy wrote home.

It was not as hard as a day at Long Lick, a country church he had pastored in Kentucky, and it was not uncomfortably hot. Already picking up the patois, he pronounced our new town "a good city plenty native good." When Mother visited the homes of the local Baptist school teachers and the pastor in the afternoon, though, she confessed she was "shocked" at what she called the "nativeness" of it—the open fire outside where everyone did their cooking, the plain rooms with one table, no chairs.

Yet a church reception a couple of days later was, she wrote, "lovely" and "mostly in English." We were served tea, cookies, and candy. In the evening, hearing drums in the distance, Mother remembered an Assembly of God missionary's talk of Ashanti headhunting (we would learn to take "missionary stories" with bushels of salt)—and the heads they were said to hunt were the heads of Yorubas from Nigeria, the people who had given us such a warm welcome. But when I asked her one night why people were drumming, she told me they were dancing, and I wanted to dance with them.

❧

In our European-style Kumasi house with proper windows and doors, Mother set about making us a Kentucky home. She remade her old college bedspreads into draperies; she painted and cleaned with the help of a cook (Rafael) and a steward (Jimah). I helped Jimah dust or made gingerbread boys with Rafael, or puttered around the bare-dirt backyard, talking to the man who had a garden there and called me "honey" because that is what Mother called me. Or I sat on the concrete cistern that held our rainwater, admiring the paw-paw tree with its big globes of yellow fruit or watching red-headed long-tailed lizards bask in the sun. One day, perched on the cistern, I had a thought—oddly associated, in my memory, with a purple cocoa tin lying against the house wall: does God really exist? One day at bedtime, I asked, "Is God here in my bed?" "Is he there on the floor?" I was full of questions. "Why does the mosquito net have holes in it?" Why are Africans happy?" "Why can't we just go back to America?"

I was only three years old, and my suitcase of expectations was not large, yet there were some things I expected. I expected to see my Aunt Eleanor, who taught first grade in Frankfort and wore bright red lipstick and stylish clothes and hats she made for herself, and I wanted to grow up to be just like her. I stood in front of her picture on a little table in the living room and cried my heart out. "I'm sad because I want to see Aunt Eleanor," I wailed. "That is what the matter is all the time."

I made Mother pretend to be Aunt Eleanor for a whole day and nearly loved her to death. I pretended to be Grandmother Claxon and cooked in the backyard like the Kumasi women. I drew a picture of Grandmother Claxon's house in Frankfort with Grandmother in the window and Aunt Eleanor and me out front holding hands. On my pretend piano, the table, I played "Mammy had a speckled hen," which Aunt Eleanor had taught me to plunk out on the black notes of Grandmother Claxon's upright piano.

Mother had an idea: I could say my own letter to Aunt Eleanor, and Mother would type the words:

There are black people at Africa. They walk without any shoes. They carry things on their heads. . . . We love them. We have toilets at Africa. We have bathrooms at Africa. The boy comes around with the bucket on his head. The bucket is to empty our toilet. He hates to walk around in the toilet, that old smelly toilet. . . . There is a little black girl named Sade. There is a little black boy named Bee. There's a sister that's named Mary. They come to see me every day. And we have a cook named Rafael and Rafael has a brother and he is named Jimah. And he cleans the house up. And he dusts the floor.

I told Aunt Eleanor I loved her. I asked if she would play the piano if I saw her. Would she let me hang up some clothes? I assured her: "I'm going to soon be back." I was struggling to connect my two worlds: the Kentucky world I knew for the first three years of my life and the African world my parents had brought me to.

✗⊙

Back in Kentucky, Grandmother Claxon worried about my not having white children to play with. "I don't like to think of her going through the hardships of life there, not knowing

With Sade in Kumasi

With Alice in our yard

With my kitten, Ginger

A rare instance of me in local dress, shown here with church ladies and a child from another mission

the pleasure of living with white children," she wrote. Daddy asked Eleanor to tell her not to worry. He said they would make a special effort to get me together with white children. And in fact, at first I did play with an American missionary girl next door. But when she moved away and I had no one to play with, Mother thought of Sade, the daughter of Pastor and Mrs. J. A. Idowu.

Brother Idowu was a Yoruba Baptist fieldworker from Nigeria who traveled with Daddy to visit churches around the country and taught Mother and Daddy Yoruba. His wife, herself a fieldworker for the Women's Missionary Union, took Mother visiting and told her how they did things here in the Gold Coast, like having babies at home on the floor. The first day that Sade came for a visit, I stood out front in a frilly dress waiting for forty-five minutes until she arrived. Although I could not speak her language and she could speak only "small-small" of mine, I chattered away and got mad if she didn't do what I said.

Daddy reported home that I was "beginning not to feel as queer with Africans." He had integrationist ideas that would have made it hard for him to get along as pastor of a white Kentucky Baptist church. He wrote his mother that some whites' un-Christian attitude toward Negroes in America was affecting mission work among Africans. He told the children he taught at the Kumasi church's primary school the story of the African-American singer Marian Anderson, who broke a racial barrier by singing spirituals at the Lincoln Memorial.

In no time, I was holding hands with Sade in church, and Mother told Daddy's family, "I think soon, she will be loving the African children just as much as the white ones." As

Mother typed her letter, Alice, who was fourteen and Yoruba, was reading a story to me and Sade and Bee—all black, Mother noted, but me. One evening after my new friends left, I prayed, "Thank you for my little friends and I hope they will be back again." They were—though after fourteen showed up one day, Mother told Mr. Idowu we could have only two at a time; it was too hard to keep an eye on them all.

A month after my fourth birthday party, Mother and Daddy were commenting on my "cosmopolitan" friendships. I had gone to a Scotch lassies' party and met Scottish children. I had been playing with a Syrian boy next door and with a couple of girls who were a mix of West African, West Indian, and white (all of unidentified nationalities). Ethnicity had never been this fluid in Kentucky, nor had we ever encountered such varieties of it. After the American mission family moved out of the other side of the house, an Englishman who worked for a drug company moved in. He did fine embroidery, borrowed mother's sewing machine to work on his draperies, and read Mother's *Good Housekeeping*, trying out new recipes on his many guests. He had a fat cat and gave me a marmalade colored Persian kitten he named "Ginger."

When he moved out, a young English couple named Elsie and Jack took his place, and soon we were all having afternoon tea together. Elsie and Jack played with me so much that Daddy said maybe I had the wrong parents. Jack made me airplanes and we sailed them in the yard. He worried when he saw me with teenage Alice bouncing on my big seesaw with our arms out, not holding on, and bumping hard. When I swung, I pumped my legs till I was almost at the top of the nine-foot frame. Daddy said I would break my neck. Mother (who had been a tree-climber herself in her youth) said I might as well break it that way as any other; I had to do something.

I was, in fact, Daddy wrote, "as busy as a bird dog." Once when he called me down from the top of the garden where I was out of their sight, I appeared, bare chested in my panties, covered with mud, and crying over the interruption as if my heart would break. "But Daddy, I was setting out a paw-paw leaf," I sobbed. "I had the little round hole all ready." Sometimes, Mother said, it was all they could do to hold in their laughter.

They were clearly proud, though—proud when I sang my one Yoruba song to the children at church, proud when someone said I talked like a dictionary, using words like "muttered" and "wept." I "read," turning the pages of books as if I understood the words—and would have read more if my parents had let me. My eyes had been badly crossed since about the age of two, and though I had glasses with prisms in an attempt to straighten my vision, one eye still turned sharply in. Following doctor's orders, my parents put a patch on the "good" eye for two hours a day and tried to restrict the time I spent looking at books, but once after Mother put away my little picture books, she found me with a stack of Daddy's theology books, turning the pages of one about the crucifixion. Clearly, I had a mind of my own. Once when Elsie next door read a story to me one way, I insisted it should be read another way. "Aunt Elsie, I'm *telling* you," I said.

I had a new aunt, a new life. In the journal he kept that year, Daddy wrote, "Carol Ann was out on road with tricycle today. Never before. I felt funny—she was perfectly at peace. 'B' Idowu with her."

Reading Daddy's journal, I see how he whose father died when he was six years old reveled in his own fatherhood. He played with me, read to me, dressed me, rocked me to sleep. He worried about me—about my health, my character. He and I both had tempers. He lost his at our cook, Rafael. I threw a "jiminy fit" over not getting my way. When I sassed him, he spanked me, and then I would ask, "Do you love me?" or would say it didn't hurt much, which could provoke harder licks. "I whipped her much," Daddy wrote once after I cried forty-five minutes when Mother went off to teach.

Mother, too, sometimes switched my legs (though she hated it when the headmaster beat the children at school), and when she was very old sometimes asked me, "Do you think we abused you when you were little?"—not, I think, seriously considering the possibility. They were, I believe, carrying on the punishment traditions of their own families; whatever emotional scars I carry, I know I was loved. "C.A. & I took a walk before supper," Daddy wrote in his journal. "C.A. said, 'I like this beautiful world.'"

Daddy had never kept a journal before and he had trouble making time for it. Still, most days he managed to jot down a small page of notes; if he missed a few days he tried to catch up from memory. He wrote about the vegetables he planted in the garden and about the books and magazines he was reading—*The Babe Ruth Story*, *Life*. He wrote about missing tennis and how happy he was when he joined the African tennis club, less expensive and easier to get to than the European club. He described telling moments, as when a European truck driver demonstrated "the spirit of overlording" by not moving

With Daddy

Women at church

Church folks with Daddy and Mother, dressed in attire given to
them by the Gold Coast Women's Missionary Union, probably on
a farewell occasion bidding us goodbye from the Gold Coast

to the side of the road to let the African bus in which we were riding go by. "No wonder the African often desires freedom," Daddy wrote at a time when Kwame Nkrumah was leading a movement for Gold Coast independence.

More often, motivated, perhaps, by the idea that these entries might be useful to him in the future or even that he was, in his way, making history, he wrote about his work traveling around the Gold Coast without a car, riding hundreds of miles in lorries. He went north where he saw the "real primitive Africa"—mud houses, grass roofs, women with nearly nothing on. He negotiated with chiefs and colonial government officials over land for new church buildings. He tried to explain to Baptist groups that wanted to transform themselves into churches why every man needed to have only one wife.

I try now to imagine what it was like for this father of mine who had not seen much of the world to make his way through the multiple cultures of the Gold Coast. When Daddy preached, he had to line out his sermons with an interpreter translating what he said into Yoruba. At times, a second interpreter joined in, repeating his words in Twi, the language of the Ashanti, dominant in this part of the country. Beyond the challenge of preaching in a foreign language, there was perhaps a greater challenge. How, he asked himself, could he write sermons for people whose minds he did not understand?

He did usually have a companion and guide on his travels—Mr. Idowu, though they would part ways for lodging at night. Mr. Idowu would stay with fellow Yorubas and Daddy would stay at a government rest house or with missionaries, although once, in Cape Coast, when the rest house was unavailable, he did stay in a church member's room. "They really did everything to make me comfortable," he wrote in his journal that night, "Bed like a rock but I slept well."

Mother, too, recorded her daily life in writing, pouring out sights and sounds on the blue air letter forms she sometimes used for her letters home. She described the local women's charm—the way "they bow when they salute you," their pretty dresses, and even prettier, their headdress, elaborately wrapped strips of cloth; how they sometimes wanted to touch her stockinged legs, and she let them.

In one letter, she invited her Mother back in Kentucky to go shopping with us. "I'll send the garden boy for a taxi, since I am about ready. Oh, dear, where is that post office key? Let's see, how many pounds will I need? I think three will be enough for the material and all. ($12.) You are not used to riding in a little car like this English one? Does it seem funny to be riding on the left side of the street? I haven't got used to it myself, yet. Sometimes I think surely we will crash head-on into someone, but we always get by."

There were dark streaks in the picture she sketched of our new life—more, I expect, than she shared in letters home, though she did mention the house staff's request to leave work early one night "as they feared much" after the chief of a nearby village had died. She was told that two, three, even four people might be sacrificed after a chief's death. She and Daddy sent the cook and steward home in a taxi.

Before Daddy left on his first trip, Mother suggested asking Mrs. Idowu to stay with us as protection while he was gone, but Daddy thought having the gardener stay on the porch would do. Mrs. Idowu herself said we should always have someone sleep at our house since, Mother wrote, ""we are too much alone and they feared thieves for us. She is a dear." There were no fellow Baptist missionaries on hand to show Mother and Daddy how to live their new lives; they were grateful to have the Idowus, who, as Yorubas from Nigeria, were themselves—in a way—foreigners like us.

Once we all took a "bush trip" with the Idowus to Ejura, sixty-five miles north of Kumasi. By Mother's account, it was a panorama of odd moments: a big snake coiled up in the kitchen drawer of the rest house where we stayed; a strange noise like an animal coming closer and closer to the rest house that night; an English public works director who sent his drunk driver to take us home after church (though the car no sooner started than it broke down and we walked back in the mid-afternoon sun). After lunch, Daddy held a short afternoon service and everyone marched to the knee-deep river for a baptismal service. We walked past the market and through a cane field, singing "Come and go with me, to my Father's house" in Yoruba, a song I already knew and could sing now, if you asked me: "Wá bá mi ká lo . . . ."

The baptisms over, the public works director who had offered us a ride earlier passed in his car with a woman who Mrs. Idowu said was probably his African wife. His car pulled up at a "hotel," a small building that looked just like any other home. Brother Idowu went to ask him if he planned to take Mother, Daddy, and me back to the rest house. He said he would. We waited. Darkness fell. "An African night can be the blackest night you can imagine," Mother wrote, "and now it was thundering and lightning and promising to pour down rain. We could look into the dimly lighted room and see the white man sitting at the table and three or four black people around. We saw them handing another bottle to him." Finally, Mrs. Idowu went to tell him the missionaries were ready to go home. He came out and said that though he was not himself a believer, he appreciated our coming as it meant much to the people. He insisted we stay with him the next time we came. He was "very gracious," Mother wrote, but "quite drunk."

Daddy's letters home were not as colorful or attuned to the drama of life, but he too told stories. There was, for instance, the rare time when he "witnessed" in the Kumasi market—a way, he thought, to reach beyond the Yorubas with whom he was mostly working. After a talk with a Muslim man, Daddy said in parting, "I will pray for you," and the Muslim replied, generously, "And I will pray for you."

✷

Our first African Christmas was approaching. Weeks before, Mother had asked Eleanor to tuck a few things into the Christmas package if she hadn't mailed it yet: foot powder for Daddy, a typing eraser, a spool or two of thread, packages of Kool-Aid, and, if she needed packing material, rags for cleaning or copies of the *Frankfort State Journal*. Mother also gave her another commission: to buy books for the children's library that Mother wanted to start at the church's school, where she and Daddy both taught. The children there had contributed

$12.50, and the church had given over $20 to buy books. Would Eleanor pick out some Little Golden Books and Tell-a-Tale books—illustrated stories that would help the children with their English, the colonial language which was, Mother explained, a "foreign language to them"? When the books came, the children made covers for them out of newspapers to make them last.

On Christmas day we opened our own packages from America—for me, red shoes, a garage with little cars, a rubber baby doll that drank from a tiny bottle and wet itself. The leaves were dropping off our Christmas tree by Christmas morning, but in a letter to his mother and sisters, Daddy laid claim to the authenticity of our Christmas, with sheep roaming the streets and people in sandals and robes, and temperatures warm enough for shepherds to sleep out on the hills and hear the angels sing.

About a fortnight after Christmas, Mother returned from the post office crying. I asked her why, but she could not speak. "Mommy, you don't always cry when you go to town," I said. She did not want to say why, but I just had to know. Finally she told me: her father, my only grandfather, had died. Grandpa Osborne had gone to be with God, Daddy said. I asked how he got there.

The days that followed were hard for Mother. She had not slept well for a long time. First she had worried about her father when he was sick. Now she lay awake thinking about him, and about her mother, left all alone on the little farm they had bought after Grandpa retired from the railroad. Mother also had more to do than she could handle. While Daddy was off on a trip, she had fired Rafael, our cook—he had broken so many things, helped himself to our food, and was, besides, not as clean as she wanted him to be. Trying to get everything done without him, she felt like she was running with her feet tied.

She was looking forward to our move to Iwo, Nigeria, where we would live on the same compound with seminary friends Carl and Enid Whirley and their son Johnny, my age. Mother would teach in the Baptist College and Daddy would help churches throughout Nigeria and the Gold Coast with their Training Unions, weekly sessions on Baptist doctrine and church citizenship—preparation, in a way, for the day when Nigeria would become independent from Britain.

While Baptist missionaries had only lately arrived in the Gold Coast and so far numbered exactly two (the ones we had replaced for this year), Baptist missionaries numbered more than a hundred in Nigeria. Living on the Iwo compound with other missionaries, my parents would not only have more fellowship but also might be able to stretch their annual salary of $1,000 farther than they had in Kumasi. New expenses had popped up with no savings to cover them. The refrigerator we had brought with us from the United States was no good; we had been without one for months. Mother had planned to use the money she had withdrawn from the Kentucky teacher retirement fund to buy furniture in Nigeria, but now she thought she would rather buy a refrigerator than furniture. We could sleep on mattresses on the floor and sit on boxes if we had to.

We would have plenty of boxes for that. We packed up thirty of them with belongings and had not a one left for my cat, Ginger, so Daddy carried her to the Kumasi train station, where she tried to run away, but someone caught her and brought her back, and Daddy made a harness for her out of his camera strap.

Before we boarded our ship in Takoradi on July 3, 1949, for our voyage east along the West African coast to Nigeria, I saw an eye doctor in nearby Sekondi. He told Mother and Daddy that I had "concomitant convergent squint." I used only one eye at a time. Instead of covering one eye, as they had been doing, they needed to give me exercises to make me use both eyes together. My glasses with their prisms were fine, though the doctor recommended getting prescription sunglasses to screen out the bright West African sun. He also suggested they take me to see a specialist in Nigeria.

And so, once we arrived in Nigeria, Mother and I flew in a little two-engine plane to see an eye doctor in Kano, in the North, where she was told there was really not much to be done for my eyes. The doctor did order an exercise device that might help, and I got two new pairs of glasses—one colored and one plain. But he said even surgery was not likely to fix my eyes. The problem was not just in the muscles: "There is no fusion of objects in the brain." It was an appropriate disability, it occurs to me now, for a girl growing up on two continents.

My parents, Emma and Neville Claxon, newlyweds in Kentucky

The Spirit That Moved Them

It would be years before I thought to wonder how my parents chose for me such a different childhood, though of course what they chose was their adulthood, or what was left of it. They were neither young nor reckless when we stepped aboard the S.S. Granville in Brooklyn on that first voyage from the United States to West Africa in 1948. Daddy was thirty-two; Mother turned thirty-six on the way.

Although I doubt they knew it, they were riding a historical wave as the United States turned its wartime might toward remaking the postwar world. Mother reported in a letter home that someone had said that at least Baptist missionaries did not want to change the culture, but, of course, they did: they wanted people to have medical care; they wanted young people to go to schools; they wanted each man to have only one wife, and they wanted Christianity to replace traditional beliefs and Islam. They were part of the Western project of modernizing the Third World.

Mother and Daddy themselves had had what an Indian scholar-friend of mine calls Third World experiences within their First World lives. Both were former Kentucky schoolteachers who had been through the school of hard knocks growing up—especially Daddy. In my living room I have a photograph taken when he was about four: Daddy, his two little sisters and his mother and father posed in the yard of their house on the rocky hill where they lived in Franklin County, Kentucky—all unaware that the axe was about to fall, that within a couple of years, Daddy's daddy would be dead of meningitis at the age of thirty-three.

I grew up to raise a child without a father just like my Grandmother Claxon, only she raised three children by herself on that little farm on a rocky hillside without indoor plumbing. She sold the car she couldn't drive and bought a carriage for the pony to pull, and when Daddy was old enough, he drove the carriage, turning it over once on the way to the Switzer church where his family worshipped in life and were buried in death. Daddy's uncle up the road farmed their tobacco allotment and Daddy helped. At thirteen, he was the man of the family. I have a picture of him in knee britches, jacket, and bowtie—proud winner of a county fair trophy for his calf, standing dignified beside him. He and his sister Eleanor took enough college courses to become teachers. Doris, the wild one, married a sailor.

Mother's family was a little more prosperous than Daddy's—and more colorful in my imagination because she told me more stories about her growing up. Daddy talked about having oranges only at Christmas because they were so poor. Mother talked about falling asleep in a haystack with her cousin after

Daddy and his sisters, Eleanor and Doris, with their mother, Frona, and their father, Elmer

Daddy with his prize-winning heifer

Mother (third from right) with friends at Eastern Kentucky University

*Daddy (left, back row) with the basketball team
he coached at Elkhorn School in Frankfort*

picking beans at Red River and climbing a tree with her brother Jimmy in Winchester and eavesdropping on passersby below and running off with her girlfriends from a neighbor's orchard with green apples bouncing in their bloomers. In Winchester her family lived in a house her mother's father bought for them—he was a Ledford who owned mountain land in eastern Kentucky, near Frenchburg, the little town where Mother was born, and made enough money farming and selling trees off his land to buy a house for each of his children.

The house Mother grew up in was on Georgia Street, where Mother sledded in winter and climbed trees in summer, while her mother planted a garden that got bigger and bigger during the Depression until it took up nearly all the space in the yard. Mother's daddy worked for the railroad. He was a stern father with clear ideas of how girls ought to behave; when he came home and found Mother riding Jimmy's bicycle or up in the tree out front, he whipped her legs with his razor strap.

Jimmy went off to college and then law school, but when Mother started classes at Kentucky Wesleyan College and asked an aunt and uncle to help her pay for her books, they turned her down because she was a girl. She worked in a dime store until she transferred to Eastern Kentucky State Teachers College, where she worked in the school cafeteria and administrative offices and took breaks from her courses to teach eight grades in a one-room schoolhouse on an east Kentucky ridge not far from where she was born. There she lived in a house with a widow who had two sons and two daughters and neither running water nor electricity. The woods were their toilet, the fireplace provided what heat there was. On cold nights Mother slept in the bed with the widow and her daughters to keep warm. At school the children gathered around a potbellied stove, sometimes joined by a neighbor who did not have all his wits about him but knew enough to come in out of the cold.

It took Mother ten years to finish college. She taught for a while to earn money for school, then took a few more classes, then taught, and so on until finally she finished her bachelor's degree in 1940 and landed a high school teaching job in Frankfort. There she met Daddy. He had been studying at Georgetown, a small Baptist college nearby, and teaching his way through the Depression for seven years when he met Mother. He was three years younger—twenty-five, meticulously dressed. She was twenty-eight, beautiful, with mysterious hooded eyes and curvaceous legs. They played tennis on their first date, and Daddy was impressed that she did not say "Gosh" or "Darn" when she missed the ball.

Mother had been in love before with a Jewish boy and had agonized over whether she could marry someone out of her Baptist faith, but after two years, she decided against it. "Needless to say," she wrote me once when I was dithering over my own love life, "I've never been sorry." She and Daddy married on August 29, 1942, when she was thirty and he was nearly twenty-seven. Daddy started studies for his master's of theology degree at the Southern Baptist seminary in Louisville and pastored country churches while she taught commerce in a nearby high school. In 1945, the year World War II ended, I was born. Three years later, moved by the spirit while Daddy was studying at the Baptist seminary in Louisville, they took me to Africa.

The spirit that moved them, I suspect, was not only the Holy one. I expect the spirit of adventure had something to do with it—the same spirit that led my mother's grandfather to pack his family into a covered wagon in the nineteenth century and move them across the country to Oregon (though, missing Red River, he soon packed them up again and brought them back by the new transcontinental train) . . . the spirit that sent my Mother by train across the country to California to visit San Jose State University and decide if she wanted to study there . . . the spirit that sent a branch of my father's family to Colorado to live and his parents to visit them on their honeymoon. There's a voice I often hear in my head: "Life has something else in store for you." I believe my parents heard that voice, too.

In today's world they might have joined the Peace Corps. In their world, they became missionaries. Daddy explained why they did in a sermon that I found in his files. His father's early death had made him depend more on his heavenly father, he said, and he came to believe that his heavenly father wanted him either to teach, like his own father, or preach, like the pastors who had been fathers to him. Church had been to Daddy growing up a haven, a home. It is not surprising that it became for him a vocation.

He had learned young the truth he preached in another sermon just two years before his own death: "Life is a vapor—a mist—a fog which lasts for only a little while and is gone... So we all must make our time count for the most. Let us stop and ask, 'What is my life? What is it worth in this world? What am I doing that is of value to God— to man—even to myself?'" Everyone, he said, should consider the needs about

Mother and me at the Empire State Building on our way to Africa

him. "It was on the basis of the great need for the gospel in Africa that Emma and I considered the call of God to go there as missionaries. We have never doubted that God was in that call." When I grew up to wail and moan about what I should be doing in life, he would say, "I don't have that trouble. I just ask God, and then I do his will."

In 1948, trust in God's will was common among Americans. Churches stood on every corner and people went to them, dropping their offerings in the plate as it came round. Not everyone had as deep a yearning for God's guidance and support as my father, but many believed, and many of those who believed held missionaries and missions in high esteem. You did not have to be a fanatic to become a missionary in 1948. You only had to take your faith seriously and be adventurous enough to leave home and live among people whose ways were strange to you.

Mother and Daddy applied to the Southern Baptist Foreign Mission Board to go to Hawaii (not yet a state) because they thought Mother's age would prevent them from going somewhere more demanding. They traveled to headquarters in Richmond, Virginia, wrote out their autobiographies, a page for each year, and saw a psychiatrist, who asked them questions, gave them inkblot tests, and concluded that whatever alternatives lay before him, Daddy took on the hardest. In 1948 the hardest thing for them both was to accept the board's invitation to go to Africa. Leaving behind ailing parents, they set off on a Norwegian ship to go halfway across the world, and they took me with them.

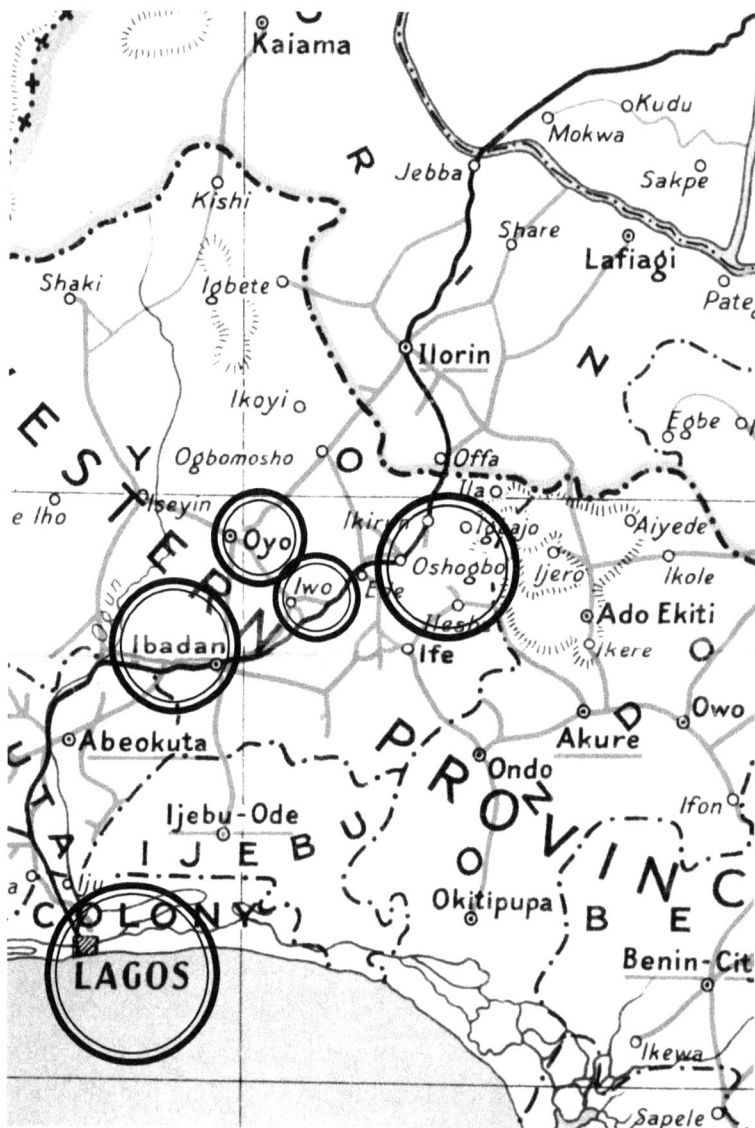

Nigeria, 1947

(*Modified detail of a map published by the Directorate of Colonial
Surveys and printed by the War Office of the United Kingdom*)

How Minds Are Made
and Unmade

Everyone, I hope, has a landscape to hold in the heart as a refuge from trying times. The Rocks at Iwo would become mine. Lying homesick in America in the years to come, I would remember that big rock hill at the edge of our yard, the cracks I jumped across with my new missionary kid friends, the steep slope we slid down again and again until we wore holes in the seats of our jeans, the fairy pools where women washed the clothes they carried balanced on their heads.

To my four-year-old self, the Rocks were a magic place, an Other World, but much of my world then seemed otherworldly to me. Elfin lights flickered along dark streets. Apocalyptic flames leaped high on either side of the car where farmers set fires to clear the tall bush grass from their fields. I climbed to the top of towering flamboyant trees by the tennis court, shinnied along the smooth trunks of guava trees to pick their pulpy fruit, plucked patanga cherries off bushes. Roger, Richard, Johnny, and I—more or less the same age—roamed the compound, our personal Garden of Eden, complete with big snakes that dropped from our trees and were shot by a missionary or pounded to death with a stick by whatever Nigerian happened by.

Sometimes a snake would make its way into the house and curl up in a kitchen drawer. Scorpions favored bookshelves. Insects we called "jiggers" could bore into our feet so that I had to wear shoes even inside the house, envying the Africans around me who mostly went barefoot everywhere. Once I stepped on a thick black line of driver ants crossing the sandy road through the compound, and, in a flash, ants swarmed over me, stinging in the most hidden places. Mojishola, a sturdy teenager who watched over me, scooped me up and hauled me screaming to Mother, who stood me on a table and stripped me down to bare skin.

There were worse things, harder for a four-year-old to understand. I gave the washman a kitten from my cat's litter, and a few days later he came back and said the wall of his house fell on it and he needed another. Our steward said not to give him a second because he had "chopped" the first. Then there was a Sunday when we came home from church to find facial marks carved on my rubber doll's face. I felt a thick thud of fear, wondering, perhaps, if whoever did that to my doll might do the same thing to me. I made Mother put my doll up high in the closet where I would never see her again. After I was grown, Mother told me she thought the facecutters were Mojishola and a houseboy. She thought they were not being mean—they just wanted the doll to look like themselves.

Moji was most of the time my best girl friend. She cooked yam on the washman's fire and gave me half. We made mud pies or spread a mat on the floor to lie side by side. Such a sight, Mother thought—long, dark Moji and little white me, side by side on the floor. We sang a Yoruba hymn together, "Layo, layo wonyi bẹ, Hallelujah," Moji singing the first words, me coming in on the "Hallelujah." Mother could not carry a tune but Moji made up for that, singing through the days, humming a song and letting me guess what it was. She showed me how to dance Yoruba-style, jigging back and forth on my two feet, shifting my weight. Mother guessed she was giving me Yoruba ideas about baby care, too, when I asked for a new doll that I could strap with a cloth onto my back.

One day I came in with a praying mantis and, in Yoruba-accented English, said, "He is not a gr ah ss – hopp ah!" Moji had pulled his legs off and was looking for a thread to tie him with. Mother hoped I would not pick up "African cruelty" as well as the accent. I have learned, of course, that Americans have their own forms of cruelty, and I am probably no crueler than most. But I wonder now what I did pick up from Moji that I am unaware of: ways of being in the world that I might value—secret selves that have slipped into the shadows. We spent hours together in a period when my social skills and patterns were developing rapidly. If I picked up her accent, did I also pick up something else?

After I grew up, an American friend would tell me I did not quite have the idiom of American social interactions down. Every now and then, he said, I missed a beat. He guessed that was because I did not grow up in America, but I did have American parents and was surrounded by Americans in the mission community—surely, enough American social interaction to learn its rhythms. But surely, too, I picked up

Yoruba rhythms—Yoruba social ways? Are they still there, a counter-tune playing dimly in the background?

Or maybe the offbeat had its source in the steady state of difference I grew up in, beginning with language. To this day, when I hear people in cafés speaking a foreign language, I feel comfort slide over me. It feels natural to walk through a world where I do not understand what strangers around me are saying and unnatural, sometimes irritating, to understand everything that is being said. Mostly what I heard outside the cocoon of family and mission life was Yoruba, surely one of the world's most beautiful languages, deeply tonal, words conveying meaning by their rise and their fall, a language as close to music as any I have ever heard.

Yet immersed in it though I was, I never learned to speak in Yoruba, only English with a Yoruba accent, and a little Pidgin English, with its distinctive accents and syntax and vocabulary: "I no go give you dees one....Dees ting cost plenty-plenty...the car it dey finish, pata pata, no good...." Living later in the United States, I had to make an effort not to speak my Yoruba English to every black person I met, and so, eventually, I lost it. For years, lying sleepless in bed, I would try to get it back, whispering words to myself in the dark, as if by recovering the sounds I would recover some part of my lost self.

✗

We were just settling into our Iwo house at the end of the compound road in August 1949 when Daddy went back to the Gold Coast to help new missionaries who had just arrived in

Our Iwo house

Picnic on the Rocks

Kumasi. Mrs. Idowu wrote Mother that Sade was disappointed that I had not come, too. When Mrs. Idowu asked Sade if she thought I would come all that way to play, Sade said "that it is not too much for two friends." But I had moved on—to a new place and new friends.

If my childminder Mojishola was my best girl friend, Johnny Whirley was my soulmate. We romped through our fourth and fifth years together like unruly lambs. At family dinners we made such a ruckus "talking and carrying on" that getting us to stop and eat was, Daddy said, like "stopping a stampede of cattle." The Whirleys—friends at the Louisville seminary before we all came to Africa—were then and forever after our best missionary friends. Daddy played tennis nearly every day with Uncle Carl on the clay court. Mother could barely stand a day without seeing Johnny's mother, Aunt Enid.

Aunt Enid was like a second mother to me—it was she who ordered a correspondence course from Calvert School in Baltimore, a source of lessons for American diplomats, military families, and missionaries in those parts of the world where local schools were not American enough for their children. I had been eager to read for a long time, but Mother and Daddy had been holding me back because, even with glasses, my eyes sometimes hurt. Once I started kindergarten, though, they gave in. I learned to read using a Calvert phonics scroll with beginnings of words on the left side and endings on the right: c-at, b-at, r-at....or d-og, h-og, l-og.

The course also came with cutouts for an American farm: pigs, horses, cows, none of which I ever saw around me except for an occasional chief's horse or the gaunt long-

Mojishola and me

Johnny and me

Roger, me, and the teepee

Cutting the grass with Johnny

horned cattle that jostled past on their way from the tsetse-fly-free North to be slaughtered for our markets. Johnny and I dutifully constructed a world we did not know, complete with a cardboard barn and cardboard ducks to swim on a mirror-pond. March arrived and the kindergarten instructions said to make a kite, so Daddy and I made one and tried to fly it in the front yard, running back and forth over the stubbly grass while the kite trailed behind. Not a breeze stirred in our equatorial March. We studied American Indians and Daddy made me a bow and arrow and tied poles together in the garden and wrapped an old quilt around them to make a teepee.

We did these American things, but Johnny and I knew we were not in America. When we dug a hole in the sandbox and one of us said, "Do you think we could dig to China?" the other replied, "No, that's if you dig from America."

Together we had entered a philosophical age. At a birthday wiener roast for my next-door neighbor Roger Congdon, I told Johnny that God did not make the plants but just the seeds. Johnny said God made the plants grow from the seeds. If I had wondered in Kumasi whether God really existed, I had no doubts now, and I knew just where he was: in my heart. He came into my heart, I told Mother, and the Devil was right behind him, "but God came in quick and closed the door and left the Devil out." When Mother and Daddy wouldn't let me drink the grape juice in those tiny glasses in church, I fell down on the road on the way home and cried. If God was in my heart, then shouldn't I, too, be remembering Jesus by taking the Lord's Supper? "Explain it to me, Mother," I demanded, as I often did.

I did not, however, always accept what I was told. One evening I reported at dinner that Johnny, Roger, and I each had favorite Bible verses that we liked to quote. Johnny always said, "I was glad when they said unto me." I always said, "Be ye kind one to another." Roger said, "Ceasing without ceasing."

Daddy said "Ceasing without ceasing" was not right. It was "Pray without ceasing."

I said, "It is right, Daddy. Aunt Esther (Roger's mother) said it was and she knows more than you. What does ceasing mean?"

"Stopping. You wouldn't say stopping without stopping."

A few minutes later, Mother and Daddy heard me muttering to myself, over and over, "Stopping without stopping—" A pause. "Daddy, did you ever go to school when you were a little boy?"

"Yes, I went all the time when I was a little boy and many years besides."

"Well," I said, "Aunt Esther goes to school now, so I think she's smarter than you."

This was our little missionary world: constant conversation around our dinner tables, blessing to the nourishment of our bodies the fried chicken or aparo—a scrawny game bird hunted by the mission men (and an occasional missionary woman), gathering to roast hot dogs on the Fourth of July, snapping English Christmas "crackers" around our casuarina Christmas trees—tugging each end until the crackers burst open with a satisfying pop, spilling out candy or a tiny toy.

One day, I opened a window on my companionable world for Aunt Eleanor, in words mother took down in shorthand and then typed.

I am going to Roger's in a few minutes. Johnny is coming over in a few minutes and he will finish his school. . . . In a few days we are going to Ogbomosho to stay a week (are we?)—to stay one day. Jim Pool is there (Are we going to stay at Jim Pool's, huh? Huh? Huh?) . . . . Mommie only has her slip on. She is in the living room. We have screens but flies still get in and Elizabeth just moved the pan with her toes. Sometimes Moji picks up stones with her toes and one day she picked up a stone with her toes and my mommy is almost finished the letter and she stops when she is ready for me to tell her more . . . . I have got plenty of flowers out of my flower bed. Some I gave to Aunt Virginia and some flowers are in a vase on the elephant table. The elephant table is polished. We have one table that is not polished. It is cracking but the one that is waxed is not cracking. Johnny is coming over here (I had better tell Roger when I go down there that Johnny is coming over here).

The table was cracking because our first dry season in Iwo had settled in. Mornings had turned chill, and Moji knitted a wool tam like her own for Mother. Harmattan winds blew dust down from the Sahara, settling thick on tables, chairs, and beds in half a day. The air was so dry that our lips cracked like the table. When we took baths we scooped the water out of the tub to flush the toilet so the cistern would not run out before the rains came to fill it up again. None of this was inconvenient to me. It was just the way things were.

But to a new missionary couple who arrived in February 1950, the conditions of our lives on the Iwo compound were such a shock that no sooner had they arrived than they cabled the Foreign Mission Board they would not stay. "They thought there would be running water in the house and 24 hr. electric service and other things," Daddy wrote his mother. "After travelling 2,000 miles, they have decided that the Lord does not want them here."

They would have to pay the board back the expenses of transporting them to Nigeria—four or five thousand dollars, he guessed. "We do not understand it and are very disappointed. The College needs them and they were rushed out because of the need." In her own letter home, Mother raised the estimate of how much they would have to reimburse the board to $6,300—they had brought furniture for the living room, bedroom, and dining room. "They feel terrible about things people have given them—said they'd repay the money." She also added a crucial detail Daddy had left out: their baby.

I try to imagine: how these young people made up their minds to become missionaries, then how their minds became unmade. All along they may have had doubts and fears that expanded when they saw their first West African towns with mud houses and open sewers. Then when they reached Iwo, population 100,000, they discovered that even in mission houses they could not turn on the lights in the daytime or twist a tap and have water come out—and germs

Iwo Missionary Kids, 1949: (l. to r.) Roger Congdon, me, Johnny Whirley, Richard Congdon, and—on the blanket—Charlotte Whirley and Robert Congdon

Missionary Kids at Mission Meeting, the one time in the year when we all got together

and ants were crawling out of the walls and scorpions lurked in bookcases and they were at least an hour's drive from a telephone or more to a hospital, and well, who knows what constituted their breaking point?

I wonder how they could have gotten this far without a clearer idea of what lay ahead. Daddy was bewildered. "There are many things to disappoint one out here but I didn't expect to find a little America," he wrote his mother. "Life is no harder in many ways and not as hard in some as I experienced in my early days." Both Daddy and Mother had known life without running water or electricity. Some of their Kentucky relatives still used outhouses and pumped water by hand in the backyard. When he was a boy, Daddy had cut grass with a scythe not unlike the cutlasses the yard-boys used in Iwo. When she taught in the mountains as a young woman, Mother had walked several miles to catch a bus home for the occasional weekend. Daddy had not had a car to drive until he started teaching. Africa was not as much of a shock to them as it might have been to some Americans.

But they, too, had a hard time getting used to some things. For months we had no couch or chairs in the living room—we had no furniture of our own at all and were using furniture borrowed from other missionaries who had gone home on furlough. There were no rugs or curtains, either. It would cost $30 to have draperies for the living room and dining room made. Mother's and Daddy's monthly salaries together came to $83, which also had to cover the salaries of a cook who made $5 a month (and ultimately quit because he said it was not enough), a gardener who made $4.80, plus a steward, a washman, and the yardboys who kept the grass cut on our couple of acres. All together, I would guess, about a quarter of our monthly income went to house staff. Mother also paid to have uniforms made for them, and she herself made dresses for Moji. Otherwise, they would just work in their dirty clothes, she said, and she was trying hard to fend off the diseases that swarmed around us—guinea worm, pinworms, intestinal disorders of all sorts.

Mother had had no experience managing servants in her American life but had started out in the Gold Coast with what appeared to be a positive attitude, laughing about small difficulties in communication—how she would send Jimah to buy oranges and he would come back with tomatoes, and she would just say, "Thank you." That was at the start. As time went on, she lost her patience. The challenge of being "madam" sucked up her energy and made her cross. The washman was so slow that she said he must be taking a nap between ironing each piece. I came in one day and told her, "You're right, Mother, the washman does take a nap. He is asleep on the table now."

Some days the cook did fine. Other times the food came to the table half done, with no salt or other seasoning. When he dried dishes with the mop rag she reminded herself not to get angry because that was how he did things at home, where even rags were scarce and water came from streams and village pumps, carried back to their houses by women and children balancing big kerosene tins of it on their heads.

By American standards, the people who took care of us were desperately poor. Once when Mother gave Moji an old pair of her underpants, Moji "just danced, she was so happy," kneeling in thanks, nearly prostrating herself in the traditional way. When Mother gave one of her old dresses to Elizabeth, a student who sometimes helped around the house, Elizabeth had it made over—"makes me feel bad," Mother said, because it was "so rotten, in shreds."

Still, knowing how poor they all were compared to us, Mother was annoyed when things in the house disappeared. What she saw as impudence was even harder for her to take, as when Daddy forgot to buy shoe polish, and our steward asked if he should use his eyes to polish Daddy's shoes. Finally, Mother and Daddy both had had enough. I filled Aunt Eleanor in on what happened: "We fired our steward & he promised to do better & we took him back & we thought we should've let him go on."

He was fired for good after he refused to take the mosquito net off the line when Mother asked him to. "Am I the one who washed it?" he asked—and then didn't move boxes both Mother and Daddy had asked him to move. They would replace him with a new steward from the East, who knew neither Yoruba nor English, only Pidgin, which Mother did not speak. Though he was willing, he didn't do as much in seven hours, Mother remarked, as his predecessor did in two. When the Whirleys eventually went home on furlough in August, we would get their steward (along with their furniture, radio, and remaining canned goods). Mother would breathe a sigh of relief: at last, a "proper boy."

*

Mother and Daddy, like their colleagues, thought they needed all this staff if they were ever to get their mission work done. Certainly, both had a cascade of duties. We'd been in Iwo less than a year when Daddy took off on a three-week trip to the East in his new black Chevrolet, bumping over roads that were either unpaved or had, at best, a tarred strip down the middle so narrow that if a lorry came racketing along crammed with passengers, chickens and yams, he had to move onto the shoulder. At the start, he drove 450 miles in two days, crossed the Niger River, and on the final lap to Joinkrama rode a few more miles in a mission jeep and then an hour in a motorboat. From there on Sunday he rode a bicycle four miles to one church where he preached, and that afternoon, took a motorboat to preach at another. During the week he taught three training classes each day—one each for church leaders, nurses, and church members: 275 in all. On his last Sunday, he preached his first radio sermon in Nigeria.

Meanwhile, Mother was teaching algebra and geometry at the college, directing the college's Training Union, and advising the staff of the literary magazine. She taught a Sunday School class, shorthand, and typing, and helped Daddy with his Training Union typing and accounts. Like Daddy she studied Yoruba (scoring top of the class in the final exam). She played "Mother, May I" with me on our front steps and read me my first chapter book—about the Little Lame Prince, who was a "splendid baby" until someone dropped him.

One day our cook told Daddy that mother was a "complete" woman. "Some of my students had told him I

On our way to the Iwo campus chapel

Students at the chapel

knew mathematics 'past' any missionary," she wrote home. "Then he'd heard Neville asking me about things like typing. He asked if I could drive a car and Neville told him a very little." The cook volunteered the opinion that she could learn in a week.

Capable as she was, her peace of mind began to collapse under her rising pile of duties. The straw that broke the camel's back came when Daddy was asked to supervise an association of churches and suggested they give the job to Mother so he could concentrate on his Training Union work. She said no. "My worst trouble here seems to be nervousness," she wrote home. "I worry too much about things, maybe because I can't do everything and see so much to do." She missed the fresh-fallen snow of a Kentucky winter, an apple tree in bloom in a Kentucky spring. After a strong rain signaled the start of the rainy season in March 1950, she wrote gratefully, "It is nice and cool this morning. Like an early June morning at home."

There was something else to lift her spirits. She and Daddy had hoped for another child—had even taken jars of baby food with them to Africa. As time passed and no second child appeared, they had given the little jars away. Now Mother, at thirty-eight, was expecting. As the rains returned, she was recovering from a rough early stretch: two months in bed at home and in the mission nursing home near the Baptist hospital in Ogbomosho, a good hour-and-a-half drive away. There is no trace of that hard time in my memory and no hint of it in the letters until after it was over—a reminder that Mother and Daddy did not tell the relatives everything.

Carrying carved wooden stools from our new car

Daddy checking his tire while I climb a tree

There is no mention in the letters, either, of an event I remember clearly: the collision between our new car and a little girl as we drove through a crowded street in Ibadan. I remember our drive to the hospital with the child and her mother in our back seat, the mother alternately fussing at the child for running into the street and wailing in fear, while my Mother covered my eyes and told me not to look. Daddy often drove injured and ill people from Iwo to hospitals in Ogbomosho or Ibadan—a child hit by a cyclist, a man who fell off a roof. This trip to the hospital with a child he himself had injured must have been agonizing for him; he had a tender heart. I never knew what happened to that child, although forever after there remained a round dent like a big dimple in the right front fender of the car—a reminder that bad things can happen to children.

By May, with Mother five months pregnant, Daddy was "in a dither." The Training Union lessons for the next half-year weren't ready yet. People who were supposed to write them had let him down. He and Mother would need to write some themselves. She finished one of them and typed another (in Yoruba) while we were at Igede, a town about ninety miles from Iwo, where red-headed six-year-old John David McGee and I doctored his cat, slid down his slide, and scrambled to the top of a wardrobe in a game of hide-and-seek. When we were in Lagos not long after, a woman told Mother she could tell I was used to playing with boys.

Mother and I went on that trip with Daddy to Lagos, Nigeria's main port and most modern city, because we both needed dental work. For several months my teeth had been in

J.O. Bamikole, Daddy's assistant and later his successor as director of the Training Union program in Nigeria

such bad shape that it was hard for me to eat food that wasn't soft. I needed five cavities filled. Remembering the pain the Lagos dentist had inflicted on me once before, I gathered little stones in the walled yard of the mission hostel and tied them up in a broken balloon to throw at him if he hurt me. In the end, I thought better of the plan and kept the stones in my pocket. Except for the dentist, I liked going to Lagos because we could go to Victoria Beach, with its long stretch of sand and giant waves and English children who ran around with nothing on. When time came for us to leave, I said, "I'll go wash," and in a minute I, too, was naked as a jaybird.

The next month Daddy was off again without us—traveling North with his assistant J.O. Bamikole and our steward to cook for them. In one week he and Mr. Bamikole visited nine churches started by Yorubas from the South. Wherever they went, they were saluted with gifts. One church gave Daddy a little snakeskin bag inscribed with his initials and Mr. Bamikole a smaller one, along with a duck and five chickens to Daddy, who bought a basket to hold them all. By the time he got home three weeks later, Daddy had driven 2,500 miles. In old age, in an autobiography that she wrote in her neat hand on slips of paper, Mother would say that "he asked the Lord, please not to let him be away from his family that long, ever again."

✳

I had little idea of the work Daddy was doing at the time, although I have more appreciation for it now that I have served on the dissertation committee of an Indiana University doctoral student, David N. Dixon, a son of missionaries in East Africa. Studying mission publishing in Kenya, Dixon suggested that it provided indigenous Kenyans an arena for at least quasi-independent discourse. Missionaries are often regarded as instruments of colonial power. Here was an argument that missionaries sometimes gave a boost to people who would eventually challenge British rule. Like the lessons Daddy published as director of the Nigerian Baptist Convention's Training Union program, the classes he taught in the churches were meant to develop leaders and citizens of churches that were essentially democratic, each church governing itself. Although the Mission Board strictly forbade missionary involvement in Nigerian politics, church governance was governance, and people were getting practice in it.

The mission policy against overt political activity was, I assume, meant to protect the mission's standing with both local and British officials, but Daddy applied it at one point to American officials as well. As he described the incident to me when I was grown, a relative who worked for the federal government in Washington, D.C., had arranged a meeting between Daddy and a Central Intelligence Agency official when we were back in the States on furlough. Because Daddy traveled so much, the CIA man wanted him to turn over maps that would, presumably, contribute to the CIA's efforts to map the world.

Whatever the reason, Daddy declined to assist and seemed proud, in the telling about it, of his decision. He knew where his priorities lay. He was working for the Lord, not for the United States. But the encounter stuck deep in his soul.

After he had the heart attack that would wind up killing him at eighty-three, in his disoriented state he believed he had to go on a spy mission and did not see how he could with all these wires connecting him to machines in the hospital. When a kind and sensible doctor told him the mission had been cancelled, he was so relieved. Only after his death did I see the double meaning the word 'mission' had in this story. He had spent three decades of his life on a 'mission' that turned out to be harder, I think, than he could have imagined. There must have been times when he wondered how he would ever manage it. With the birth of my brother, a long stretch of such a time was about to begin.

⁊ℴ

Like the Little Lame Prince before the fall, my brother, Billy, was "a splendid baby." He came in a flash on September 8, 1950. Mother was anesthetized for my birth but wide awake for his. During her recovery, someone brought her a peach that had arrived in Lagos on a boat from England. All day people drifted into her room to smell her peach, which finally she shared with just Daddy and me.

She also had a bath, only the second in a month because our cistern in Iwo had run nearly dry. While she regained her strength, Daddy changed Billy's diapers, washed some of her things, and kept an eye on me. He also tracked down information on Billy's citizenship status because, Mother wrote, "we want to be sure he's an American and not an African!" Arriving back in Iwo with new brother Billy, we were welcomed by the Reverend Bamikole, his wife, and our house staff—all standing on the front steps as if they were indeed welcoming one of their own. The house was shining, with bouquets scattered all around.

In the days to come, Billy was happy and healthy, too young yet to have the array of immunizations the rest of us had had, although he was given atabrin to protect him from malaria—a good thing because once Daddy counted seventeen mosquito bites down his little arm. Breastfeeding lowered his vulnerability to some of the diseases around us, and Mother boiled his water and washed his diapers herself to be sure they were really clean.

"It seems something happens to about every other baby out here," she wrote home, but so far, Billy was in the pink of health—gaining weight, pushing himself around his crib. I myself got sick while Daddy was off on a month-long trip to the East, and I ran a low fever for days, but my favorite missionary nurse was gone and Mother was afraid to let the Nigerian nurse give me a penicillin shot. Mother had apparently "let Moji go" back in July, but now when I was ill and said I wanted Moji, she sent for her. "Oh, how happy they are to be together again," Mother wrote.

Then in late November when Billy was three months old, our whole family set off together for a week at another mission station where Daddy preached a revival. When we got back to Iwo, a letter from Aunt Eleanor awaited us: Daddy's mother was very ill.

In just about every letter Daddy had written his mother, he had said he prayed to God to keep her safe so he might see her again. Now the moment he had feared had

Carl and Enid Whirley with their children, Charlotte and Johnny

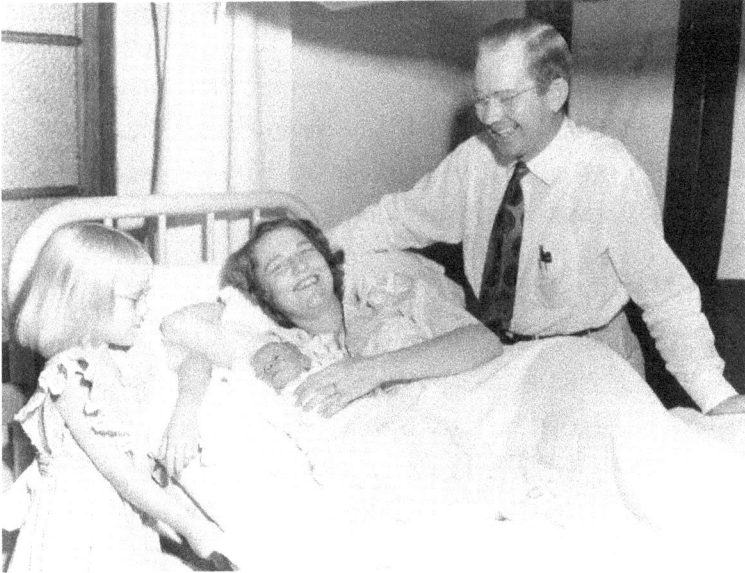

We Claxons with newborn Billy

arrived. On December 23 he sent a Western Union cable to Aunt Eleanor— "SEND WIRE IMMEDIATELY TELLING MOTHERS CONDITION LOVE=NEVILLE." He and Mother started trying to organize their work so we could fly back to the United States, but within just a few days, a runner brought another letter with the news: Grandmother Claxon had died on Christmas morning.

Even now I can see my father: stretched out on the bed in my parents' bedroom, one arm thrown over his eyes. I hover at the door, not sure what to do, what to say. I can see him as plainly as if I am in the moment again. I go to him and put my arms around him, kiss him on the cheek—feel his despair.

❧

"Sometimes," Daddy wrote his sisters after their mother's death, "it seems that the price has been too dear when we think of Emma's and my own loss in one short tour in Africa. But the promise that he 'will go with us always' gives us courage to go on." He asked for their prayers, "Our baby is sick…."

It seems something happens to about every other baby out here, Mother had said, and now something had happened to ours. He had diarrhea and his bowel movements were spotted with blood. He lost weight. He was not yet four months old. Mother was giving him glucose and might put him on a bottle to see if that helped. Doctors said they would try one thing and if that didn't work, they would try another. When his stomach hurt, he cried, and I stood by his crib and cried with him, and the cook and steward would say, "Please ma'am, the baby's crying."

After the doctors treated him with sulfaquanadine, he seemed better. Daddy had work to do for a few days in Shaki, a town well off the beaten track, and he took me with him. There, for a change, I had a girl to play with: Gita Richardson, who would always remember that before I went to bed every night, my Daddy made me Ovaltine, a British chocolate drink that sweetened the powdered milk we drank.

Back in Iwo, we found Billy sick again, so we drove to Ogbomosho, where Billy and Mother stayed for two weeks while he started a course of auromycin for what they were now diagnosing as amoebic dysentery. Mother blamed a careless mission nurse who had picked him up without washing her hands. After he finished the auromycin he was better, but not well. He hardly slept at all during the day and a lot of the night. Mother was worn out and struggled to prepare for her classes. Shadows fell right and left across our little world. A bush fire surrounded our house and there was soot everywhere. A few feet from our kitchen Daddy shot a cobra that had escaped from the fire.

Then, miraculously, Billy seemed to be well and was laughing again. The auromycin had apparently worked. He gained weight, and Mother thought he felt good enough to go to sleep by himself so she tried letting him cry—except then I cried, too, and worked myself into a state. Even if he went to sleep, he woke up again in half an hour. Finally, she gave up and rocked him. Despite it all, Mother wrote, he was "a determined little fellow." He climbed out of his high chair, and when we had a picnic in our yard, he kept crawling off the quilt she had spread for him. One day when he was chattering away, I said, 'Yes, Billy, you're going to be a preacher.'"

Mother thought my affection for him was sweet, but there were times I tried her patience. I had turned into a piddler, taking forever to get through meals and keeping myself awake at bedtime with streams of questions: "Why does a boy's bike have that piece on it in the middle?" "Can you buy everything but furniture and groceries in a 10-cent store?" When she fussed at me and Roger for eating beans from a shrub, I said, "Oh, Mother, we've been doing this for years." I ran errands around the compound on my new bicycle but preferred riding hers. When she had to dismount to push her bike up the slight hill to the house, I took it over and peddled right up, looking like "an ant on an elephant."

Still, I was thin, and my stomach sometimes hurt. She was glad we would all be having medical checkups when we got home. Already we were making plans to leave for the States at the end of May, and it was a good thing. My teeth were a mess. There were times I could not chew without crying; Mother and Daddy considered trying to go home early just to get them fixed. The dentist in Lagos had pulled one and I had three more to be filled. Mother herself lost a filling. Daddy fell on his bicycle and hurt his back. Daddy and I both had sore eyes. A refrain runs through the letters: "We are so tired."

On May 24, 1951, we flew on a four-engine propeller BOAC plane out of Lagos, bound for London so that Mother and Daddy could attend the Baptist World Congress. We stayed in suburban Twickenham with three Baptist ladies who told us about the blitz in World War II—how they might be standing in an upstairs bedroom when the sirens sounded and just had

Staying with a family in England on our way back to the United States

On furlough, a visit to Daddy's home church—North Fork Baptist Church, Switzer, Kentucky

to hold their breath and hope a bomb would not drop on top of them. Now life in their semi-detached house was peaceful and calm. There were roses in the garden and goldfish in a pool.

On the last lap of our flight home, somewhere between London and Shannon, Ireland, most of us were sleeping in the deep comforting hum of the plane's engines when a steward tied a rope around his waist and the other end around the underpinnings of Daddy's seat. The plane door was coming open, he explained, and he was about to fasten it more securely. If it were to fly open, he would be sucked out if he were not attached to Daddy's seat. Daddy sat there, his seatbelt undone, and wondered: "What then would happen to me?"

I remember the moment: the heavy hum of the plane's engine, the steward moving about in the half light of the plane, the deep dark of the night sky beyond.

❦

Life in Louisville was to me like life in a storybook. That summer, I strolled from our seminary apartment across a clovery field into the air-conditioned student center where I bought popsicles, cherry red. In fall, I would walk home from school on a sidewalk littered with large red and yellow magnolia leaves, which I picked up and stored in a box under my bed until they turned brown and crumbled. Winter would blow in, and I would slide on a borrowed sled down seminary hill, which in spring would be sprinkled with violets.

Classes had not yet started at George Rogers Clark School when I first walked with Mother into the classroom to meet the teacher and saw something I recognized: a picture I had studied in my kindergarten correspondence course. "The Little Stuart Boy," I announced. When the teacher found out I could already read, too, she sent me on to second grade where, on my first day, the teacher told us to write a theme and illustrate it with a picture. An undersized wisp of a blonde with round glasses, I approached her desk on the brink of tears. "I don't know how to write a theme," I whispered, a catch in my throat. She fixed her stern eyes on me and said kindly, "Just draw a picture then." I drew butterflies fluttering over a green hill, a picture not of anything I had ever seen but borrowed from some book or other I had read: an American picture for an American classroom.

I was odd girl out in second grade: other girls had to coach me on how to hit the punch ball at recess. "Pretend it's your brother's head!" they shouted, and I flinched at the thought. When other children found out I had grown up in Africa, they would ask curiously what it was like, and I would hardly know what to say. How could I sum up Africa or a childhood there in a few words? While for Americans, Africa was exotic, for me America was: sidewalks and television sets and the blinking neon Oertels 92 sign on Broadway in Louisville. "Have you ever seen so many tall buildings?" a relative in Chicago asked me as we rode a bus through the downtown. I stuck out my lower lip and said, "Sure, we have them in Louisville." But we didn't have them in Africa.

There was, of course, another America, not yet bursting into the future. Mother's mother lived by herself in the country in a worn-out little frame house with linoleum on the floor and stone steps up the steep bank from the country road. Daddy's

Aunt Sarah lived on a fancy farm with pink petunias by the back door, but his Aunt Nanny lived with Uncle Forrest and their two slow-witted boys in a cold house on a rocky hillside just down the road from where Daddy grew up. In 1951, she was still trekking out to the outhouse to do her business. I felt like a tourist there on that farm—standing in Uncle Forrest's dark barn where tobacco leaves hung in rows or sitting on the porch swing, studying Aunt Nanny's little feet, laced up in her black shoes and crossed neatly at the ankles, her soft light summer dress flowing down her thin body, her voice as thin as her body, a little girl's voice grown old.

While I was taking in American life, my little brother struggled with unending colds piled on top of the amoebic dysentery that kept him living on Jello. Mother and Daddy thought he might do better in warmer weather, so in the depths of winter, while Daddy stayed on at the Southern Baptist seminary to work on his doctorate, Mother, Billy, and I moved to West Palm Beach, where we lived in an apartment on a street lined with comfortingly familiar palm trees. I rode a city bus to school by myself, nervous about whether I would know where to get off but exhilarated to be out in the world on my own. Billy did feel better in balmy Florida, and I wanted to hug him all the time, cute and cuddly in his cowboy vest with his naked stomach popping out underneath.

Meanwhile, I had my own health issues. I had a tonsillectomy and, finally, eye surgery performed by a doctor in Chicago, an authority on strabismus. I went around with my eyes covered for what seemed like a long time but never doubted I would see again, which I did, although one eye still wandered inward and I could not focus with both eyes. I would not understand what that meant until my early 20s when an ophthalmologist told me I had no depth perception. The world looks flat to me, like a picture. My brain long ago gave up the struggle to fuse two images coming in at such different angles and learned to focus with only one eye at a time, leaving the other eye to take in whatever it could as peripheral vision.

I wonder if the outcome might have been different if we had not been on the missionfield, if I could have had the close observation by doctors that journal articles of the time recommended, if the doctors I did see in those early years had moved more aggressively to early surgery and then therapy. My parents did what they could. During our next year in Nigeria, Daddy would take me to see an eye doctor in Kano, and the Chicago doctor who did my surgery would examine my eyes when he visited Nigeria a few years after that. I would wear glasses with prisms. I would put drops in my eyes. None of that was good enough.

But many other children in the United States and millions in Africa failed and still fail to get any treatment for eyes like mine. In the end, a second operation when I was grown could not restore depth perception, but my eyes at least looked pretty straight and I could stop wearing glasses. There is no point feeling sorry for myself now for any price I might have paid for my parents' mission work, though I don't mind feeling sorry for Billy, whose amoebic dysentery kept its grip on his young life. In October 1952, when we sailed on a ship again for Nigeria, the illness he had lived with for most of his two years went with him.

*On a street of a West African city, probably during
a stop along the coast en route to Nigeria*

In My Own World

Walking on sidewalks in Louisville I would think: we are here now, but over there is Africa. And then we would be standing at the ship's rail squinting to watch the sea's horizon thicken into a dark line of trees, and in no time at all we would be riding inland down a ribbon of tarred road through the bush toward Oyo, less than an hour northwest of Iwo. We were to live in Oyo not because we needed to be in Oyo but because a house was available for us there: an old two-story plastered mud house without electricity or running water. While Daddy had his office on the unfinished ground floor, we lived in the second story and when Billy ran across the floor, the house shook so much that Grandmother Claxon's clock on its narrow shelf worked its way to the edge and fell off.

I loved this old house with its Aladdin lamps lit at night and its long screened porch and my own special spot there for my dolls' little beds, but for Mother, the house was a nightmare. Things crept and crawled—ants, roaches, scorpions. One day the steward killed a rat on the pantry table. That night in the kitchen hundreds of big sugar ants covered the kitchen table and shelves. Roaches swarmed the safe and wiggletails swam in the pans of water under the legs of the cabinets.

The delight Mother had taken in our African life when we arrived in Kumasi four years earlier had drained away. Instead of chatty descriptions of street life, her letters home chronicled a succession of missionary guests and the American meals she served to them—potato salad, sandwiches, pickles, chocolate cake. When the president of the Baptist World Alliance visited Oyo, Mother mimeographed the program and decorated the church. She saw that potted plants and palm branches and chairs were set in the right place. She prepared refreshments. She tried to be a model 1950s American housewife in a house where all water and waste had to be carried up and down stairs. She worked and worked and never caught up.

The stress of all this wore her down—and there was more. All of us had to have rabies shots after a dog running loose at a picnic turned to be rabid. Billy was still sick with amoebic dysentery, and Mother often stayed up much of the night with him, then in the morning she felt awful. She was going in so many directions—taking care of the garden and keeping an eye on our steward, the washman, the yardboy, and Billy's babysitter, Deborah. There were Training Union letters to type, account books to keep, my studies to monitor, and the everyday struggle to keep this wretched house clean.

All the time, too, she worried because she thought this would likely be my last tour in Africa. That was the way it was: when missionary kids turned eleven or twelve, they stayed in America with relatives to go to an American school and become true Americans. Unaware of this prospect, I lived life to the hilt on the Oyo compound. I blew on the coals of the fire the washman left in the yard until they flared into flame. I hung by my legs at the top of the frangipani tree. I made mud dams with Billy in the driveway after the rain. I drew up a plan for a "hideout" in the koto, our garbage dump: first a hole, then a right-angle turn underground for a tunnel and sticks as rafters to hold the roof up. When the hole was not even as deep as my head was high, I got tired of digging and found another hideout, readymade: a bushy bower where new shoots had sprung up from the roots of a great fallen tree.

My world was full of wonder: milky sap from the frangipani turned brown on your clothes, a chameleon changed his shade when you set him on colored paper, white ants built towering castles. An entire city of red-and-black bugs swarmed under a spreading mango tree, and Marvin Garrett, missionary principal of the Baptists' Oyo high school, paid me to collect them for a biology class he taught. I went to work packing bugs into jars by the dozens. Happily I imagined them recreating their busy lives in bug cities inside his classroom. Days after I turned them over to him, he told me, with not an ounce of regret, that the students had dissected them.

My adventures outdoors are clear in my memory in a way that my schoolwork was not, though every day I did it, following the teacher's guide to my Calvert course, writing out my little essays or doing my sums, or curled up in an armchair reading a chapter book that came with the course: *Smiling Hill Farm*. The story of a pioneer family that wound up in the automobile age, *Smiling Hill Farm* introduced me

Our playground—the frangipani tree

to the idea of history, of change over time. I already had an idea of the past, of course. Bible stories took place there: Noah and the ark, Jacob and his ladder. Calvert had brought me art prints of European kings, queens, and princes side by side with Indians and pilgrims. But these were isolated stories, disconnected. *Smiling Hill Farm* caught me up in the sweep of history—in America.

It did not occur to me to wonder about the history of Oyo. African life floated timeless around me—surely it was as it had always been? Did kingdoms and empires rise and fall? Were fortunes built? Conflicts stirred? What did I know of this? Nothing.

I did not, I think, even see the parallels between the way we lived in Oyo and the American frontier ways I read about in *Smiling Hill Farm*. I helped Mother pick cucumbers in the giant patch she had planted for pickling. I squatted near the washman's fire while he heated water for the wash. But tapping Indiana trees for maple syrup and collecting nuts in the forest seemed more romantic to me. I longed to walk in American woods. Our "bush" with its thick trees tangled up with understory was an impenetrable jungle that you'd need a cutlass to hack through unless you found one of the narrow paths villagers took and to and from their compounds. When we drove down the road, I could see them emerge from the trees bearing large loads of firewood on their heads to sell. I never walked with them.

To a degree many American eight-year-olds of 1950s suburbs could not imagine, I was confined day-to-day to a small space: our compound of four mission houses, only one besides ours containing someone for me to play with: another MK girl who was six to my eight and lacked my taste for climbing trees. She had no idea at all of how much fun it would be to eat lunch up in the frangipani tree, although when I tried to eat a pickle hanging upside down by my legs and the juice ran into my nose, I saw her point. Mostly I stuck to myself, roaming the compound or practicing my one hymn on the piano that came with the house: "I gave my life for the-e-e-e, my precious blood I shed." Or I sat on the screened porch reading comic books from the States—Lone Ranger, Lash LaRue, or the Sunday comics that arrived as stuffing in the Christmas boxes that Aunt Eleanor mailed off from Kentucky in October—Blondie, Nancy, Dennis the Menace, Mary Worth, Rex Morgan, MD.

Or I wound up our record player and put on the *Nutcracker Suite* Aunt Eleanor had sent me— "Hark to the woodland call, Come to the waltz of the flow-ers." I liked it so much that I determined to produce a dance to it at the mission meeting, that week during the year when all the missionaries in Nigeria and the Gold Coast got together in one of the Nigerian compounds. One night was devoted to fun, and I planned to contribute. We children would all wear costumes and become pansies and roses, and we would dance. Mother worried in a letter to Eleanor that this would be both impossible to pull together and on top of that "inappropriate," but she hated to disappoint me. She asked if Eleanor could find a simpler script that would do for a children's performance, and she did, but it was so unmemorable that we either did not try to put it on or I have forgotten it.

We stayed in Oyo for only about a year, but that time stands out in my memory so clearly that I believe something important happened there, and I think I know what it was: I was creating for myself an alternate world. No matter that I still played near Daddy in his office under our living quarters. What I was playing took me off to England, to the coronation of young Queen Elizabeth: I donned a crown, held a scepter, walked in stately tread across the dirt floor. I was inching away from Africa, where I was beginning to see I did not belong.

I saw not long ago a wistful painting by Carolyn Pool, a fellow Nigerian missionary kid a little older than me: two little girls looking on from a bridge while Yoruba women and their children bathe and frolic in a river below. Posting "Yoruba Bath Dream" on a Facebook page where Nigerian MKs—as we still call ourselves—keep up with each other, Carolyn said, "the two girls are my sister and me, never allowed to join in the fun." That had not been my experience in the Gold Coast, before we became absorbed in mission life, but more often than not it was my experience in Nigeria.

While missionaries worked side by side with Nigerians in hospitals, schools, and churches, we lived our personal lives on what, for Nigeria, were small estates with croton hedges and grassy lawns. Aside from annual Christmas dinners for my father's two Training Union assistants and their families, my family rarely got together with Nigerians on social occasions. The distance was maintained by both sides, as I realized when I read a letter in which Mother said, "the Africans in Nigeria don't ask us to eat with them except in rare cases (such as someone who has been in America or England and lives more or less as we do)."

The divide between us was not easily breached. Whatever efforts individual missionaries made to reach across it, there were mission taboos against too much togetherness. When the only single male missionary I knew wanted to live in a house in town among Nigerians instead of on a mission compound, he was told he could not. In response, he built a unique house of his own on the Oshogbo compound: a stone house that was round, as houses were in some parts of Nigeria. He was an architect and the house was beautiful—but the butt of jokes in the mission.

Huddling together in a foreign place is not unique to missionaries; immigrants often do it, clutching their native identities around them for psychic safety. Bound by a common purpose and employment in the same enterprise, missionaries created communal lives cemented by their American-ness. Whatever state they were from—even Texas, flush with oil money that splashed into Texans' living rooms in the form of fancy furniture and set them apart—Baptist missionaries came, in a sense, from the same village: they were all American and mostly southern. They could talk easily to one another over Kentucky fried chicken, discuss the latest news brought by the Voice of America or *Time*, exchange recipes from *Good Housekeeping*, give each other Bobbi permanents.

In what to new missionaries was a starkly alien world, they made themselves feel at home. Although a few missionaries went farther down the path into African life than others, most defined themselves daily, hourly, as American. I was surprised

A rare plunge in a river with missionary Virginia Mills and Billy

Roadside picnic: with Mother, Billy, and missionary Raymond Brothers

Billy and playmate he no longer remembers

A house by the side of the road

when I found a note Mother jotted down about our first service in Kumasi, when everyone around us was black and there we were, white, and yet, she said, she felt like one of them. That feeling passed, I believe, with our move to Nigeria, where most of the time we would be set apart with other missionary families on compounds.

Nigerians, too, had their compounds, and their own reasons for keeping their social distance. It takes energy to maintain relationships with people of a different culture, especially when their native language is not yours. You might make the effort if ambition, faith in God, or need for money required it. But you might be happy enough to let the foreigners be foreigners. And we were, still and always, foreigners, however long we had lived in Nigeria. We would live there for a while, and eventually we would go "home."

Aside from whatever lasting influence their church work had, missionaries had no real say in the country's future. This was not South or East Africa, with their substantial populations of white settlers insisting on their right to belong. Equatorial West Africa, the white man's graveyard before antibiotics and immunizations, had never been attractive to European settlers. American missionaries in Nigeria did not claim to be white Africans. They were Americans. And there were not many of them. Whatever superior airs these white people might put on over the people they called "natives" (a word that suggested both inferiority and belonging), there were not enough white people of any nation to set the tone for the country or stir the kind of resentment stirred by white settlers on some other parts of the continent.

Even before Nigeria became independent in 1960, we always knew it was Nigerians' country; the end of British rule was in sight. Meanwhile, the British ran the country through local leaders in an arrangement referred to as "indirect rule"—a system that undermined traditional governance and kept real power in British hands but eliminated the need for large numbers of Brits on the scene. The few Englishmen around were often single or left their wives at home. If they had children, they sent them back to England to reappear at Christmas, pale faced and thin, shorts and dresses riding high up their legs because they were left over from their last tropical Christmas. We white missionary children, living there year round, were rare birds.

When we passed villages in our cars, children stood in their bare dirt yards and shouted sing-song, each syllable long and drawn out and jubilant: "Ay-bo, Ay-bo," as if we were the circus come to town. I was told "ay-bo" (spelled "oyin-bo") meant "peeled skin," which made sense but was not very attractive. A scholar of the Yoruba language would one day tell me that according to Ile-Ife mythology, all the world's people were created black in Ile-Ife, and those who migrated out of Africa had their skin peeled off by a wind. Whatever the explanation, we were distinctly odd. If we stopped our car in a village, children crowded around us, laughing at me and my oyinbo brother. They leaned into the car to touch us. If we closed the windows to shut out their groping hands, they flattened their noses against the glass and peered in at us as if we are monkeys in a cage.

Like our compounds, our car set us apart in our Nigerian life. Carless in Kumasi, we had walked or taken taxis and lorries, moving among the people there as if we belonged. Now we passed them by: men, women, and children walking barefoot along the road under loads of long firewood, women pounding yam in red dirt yards, smiling round-bellied children. I did not know then that the children had stomachs like big balloons because they ate too much starch and not enough meat. I saw our house staff eating their lunch of fu-fu or slices of giant yams cooked over the coals of an outside fire and, to my mind, a tasty treat. I had no idea what it would feel like to live on fu-fu and yams, with only occasional chicken or goat stew sprinkled over the top.

I could not begin to imagine, really, the lives the vast majority of people around me lived in a state of otherness normalized by being constantly there, like the drums whose steady music accompanied the nights. Here in my Nigerian world, two categories of human beings lived sharply distinct ways of life side by side. They went barefoot, slept on mats on the floor. We wore shoes, slept in beds. While their children's bellies swelled with kwashiorkor, we went through the pleasant paces of our imitation Euro-American lives (although when my dolls fell ill, they had leprosy, fever, worms). It would be years before I would reflect on the psychological climate of growing up in a state of difference.

I am afraid the effect on my moral character was not good. Sitting in the interminable Sunday morning services, wedged with Mother and Billy into a tight row of women in stiff organdy blouses and dangling gold earrings, I thought I would die of boredom while the Yoruba sermon droned on and on. Hot, thirsty, stifling in smells and heat, I sometimes imagined that I rose from my pew like an angel and soared over the heads of the crowd, who looked up at me in awe.

While I imagined myself an angel, Billy sat in the pew next to Mother, watching her draw stories in stick figures to keep him quiet. He wanted one story again and again: the true story of a driver who wrecked his lorry and was so afraid that the passengers would beat him up that he ran off into the bush dripping blood. Mother drew the drops of blood trailing after him, drip, drip drip. At night, in an inclusive spirit that I now altogether lacked, Billy prayed, "Thank you for corn on the cob and yam and Mommie and Daddy and the broken lorry and the people and the broken glass and the blood and the driver that ran into the bush….."

Billy had barely turned three when he fell sick again while Daddy was off traveling. Uncle Marvin Garrett took us to Ogbomosho and told Mother she should stay in Ogbomosho until the doctors made Billy well. If they couldn't do that, he said, she should take him to Dr. I.N. Patterson, head of the mission, and say that she would take him home to the States where something could be done for him. Uncle Marvin had done a lab test and could see Billy's amoeba still thriving. He was losing patience with the doctors. When we arrived in Ogbomosho, the doctor gave little sign of caring about him at all. "If it were I," Uncle Marvin said, "I would turn around right now and go back home. I'll take you to the English doctor in Abeokuta." He told Mother if they fooled around and let the amoeba get into Billy's liver, Billy would be an invalid the rest of his life. Mother did not take his advice,

Billy and Jacob Madaki, a student who watched over him

and the Ogbomosho doctor started a new round of medication with plans for another course every few months.

Then shortly after that Ogbomosho trip, when we were at the 1953 mission meeting in Shaki, Billy had a bad attack of what Mother thought was bronchitis. For that he was treated with sulfa, penicillin, a shot of adrenalin, Benadryl, and other pills specifically for bronchitis. The mission doctor treating him asked Mother and Daddy why they had brought him back to Nigeria in the condition he was in, though she also told them that we could go ahead with our plans to travel to the Gold Coast where Daddy was filling in for missionary Homer Littleton for a short while.

From Kumasi, Mother wrote Eleanor in some bitterness, "You know he was sick before we came home and it seems the drs. should have advised that we have a special check-up for him. This dr. said it seemed they would have found his trouble at home. We try not to think too much about it or be too annoyed with our drs., for we are at their mercy. Of course, please don't mention any of this to anyone. But I was practically on my way home a week or so ago. I really do get discouraged. What time Billy wasn't crying, I was. Ha. Anyway, if he doesn't soon get straightened out, you may look for me and the children. Of course we would stay in New Orleans for all the check-ups, etc. [Tulane University had a Tropical Medicine Center]. But let us hope he will soon be all right. The English dr. here may help." The English doctor in Kumasi did help: he took an X-ray and ran other tests and discovered Billy had a tapeworm, which he treated. He diagnosed the bronchitis as asthma. If it turned out to be chronic, Mother wrote, we might have to come home. She declared herself about ready.

Her spirits revived during our month with Daddy in the Gold Coast. She took me to our first movie in Africa—*With a Song in My Heart* starring Susan Hayward. We had teas and dinners with old friends of varying nationalities and gave a dinner for church leaders, eighteen in all, serving "African food: black eyed peas, rice, and 'soup' … made of tomatoes, peppers, onions, and meat." We visited a gold mine and someone took my picture holding a lump of gold worth $10,000. The Littletons arrived—the family we had filled in for in 1948; briefly, I had Esther to play with while Billy played with snails he found in the yard. The house had a rediffusion box that played music delivered via a wired network, and Billy put on his clown suit and I my ballet dress that Aunt Eleanor had sent, and we danced, while Mother typed up a letter for a gardener who could not read or write. We rode a sleeper train to Takoradi on the coast for a local leave, the vacation we were due once a year. "We hope it will help Billy," Mother said, "and us all."

We stayed in another mission's guest apartment and went to the beach for three or four hours in the early mornings and late afternoons, turning brown in the sun. Daddy wrote home that Billy had been "nearer well" on the coast than he had been for three months. Before we left the Gold Coast, church leaders and Mr. Littleton asked Daddy to move there for good, but having taken on the job of directing Training Union work in both Nigeria and the Gold Coast, he meant to keep it. So back to Nigeria we went—to move yet again when other missionaries claimed the Oyo house: this time to the big city.

With Mother and Billy at Tarqua Bay and Victoria Beach

Half a Magic Hour

Even today, if you were to look at the earth from out in space you would see that while the continents of Europe, North America, and Asia are lit up like neon signs, most of Africa is still a dark continent. In Nigeria we lived under what astronomers call "dark skies," although of course they were lit by billions of stars we could actually see because the earth around us was not illuminated by electricity. I was so accustomed to dark nights that after we moved to Ibadan in November 1953, I was awed by the city lights spread out around Mapo Hill like a starry sky.

Nearly half a million people lived in Ibadan—it was then the world's biggest black city, and it pulsed with electric life. Barbers cut hair in blue rooms lit by bare bulbs. High life music blared from radios and rooftop clubs. Big and electrified though it was, Ibadan was laid out like a traditional town. Unpaved alleys and paths connected networks of family compounds while a few paved streets tied the whole thing together. Wastewater ran off down uncovered ditches. Crippled children and adults with stubs for arms and legs sat outside the doors of shops, begging. There was a sprawling market where Mother and I made our way through piles of mangoes, tomatoes, oranges, bananas, yams, okra to the tune of women's voices calling out to us as we passed. At Kingsway, an English-owned department store with aisles cleared and calm, Nigerian salesgirls stood demurely behind counters stocked with bath powder and perfume.

To the excitement of this new urban world was added another novelty: in Ibadan I had a girl my age to play with: Ann Eaglesfield, a year older and a foot taller than me. Mother once expressed doubt in a letter that Ann and I had much "fellowship," and, true, we were not really (as Anne of Green Gables would say) "kindred spirits," but we did put on a play together, draping each other in sheets to transform ourselves into statues. Or were we Romans? The details are vague, but the memory of our camaraderie is not. Glad for me to finally have company almost my own age, Mother wrote, "It was beginning to get bad at Oyo. She entertains herself well, but I could tell she missed playmates."

We had moved into a new house meant for missionaries who worked at the Baptist Press, which published lessons for church organizations like the Training Unions my father worked with. Ann's father ran the press, and she lived close enough for us to walk back and forth, though we had to cross a busy road where, inspired by women selling roadside wares all over town, I set up a stand one day to sell wild greens I had picked off the compound, but even with old Christmas cards as a bonus I sold nothing at all, and the people who passed by laughed at me.

What a distance I would have had to travel to become part of African life! I was indelibly foreign and could not even pretend to belong: pale-skinned and blonde, I would always be visible. In a rebellious moment, I imagined running away from home, but however American children in books might manage that, I had not a chance in Nigeria. I would barely get my white self down the road before I would be spotted and returned to my parents.

We had been settled in Ibadan just a few weeks when the annual Harmattan winds swept dust down from the Sahara and tumbled Billy into life-threatening bouts of asthma. Now began a search for air Billy could breathe without choking. We found it at Tarqua Bay, a cove on an island in Lagos harbor where ocean breezes blew the air clean. While Daddy returned to work in Ibadan, Mother, Billy, and I stayed in a guesthouse owned by a shipping line. We fell asleep at night to the whisper of casuarina trees, the gentle thud of waves on the shore. The bay was calm enough for swimming, the beach quietly ours.

Billy was fine at Tarqua Bay, blessedly well, but when we returned to Ibadan a few weeks later, he plunged into an asthma attack so bad that Mother held him through the night, tears rolling down her face. To her dying days, she would remember that time, and tell me again and again what she said in despair: "Lord, you gave him to me, you can take him away." A doctor came to the house and fixed up a steam tent, and a new medicine helped him pull out of this bout, but mission doctors recommended that we move to Lagos for three months to get him out of the Harmattan dust.

Thus, starting in March 1954, the month after I turned nine, we divided our family life between two towns. Mother,

Going to Tarqua Bay

Billy, and I, along with Ginger and her four kittens, would live in Lagos, while Daddy traveled or stayed wherever he could find a bed. Standing in for him with us would be our steward, Joseph Akinola—a tall, handsome Yoruba who left his own wife and baby behind in Ibadan to cook, clean, and wash clothes for us in Lagos. We rented a spacious apartment from the British Church Mission Society— a "wonderful place," Mother wrote, with parquet floors and next door, a hotel where Billy and I could sip cokes at outdoor tables.

Lagos was the closest we could come to modern urban life in Nigeria. Stately white government buildings lined the road along the marina. A Kingsway department store had a book section and a café where we ate sausage rolls and ice cream blocks with chocolate, vanilla, and strawberry lined up in a row. We could catch a taxi to Victoria Beach, its hard surf pounding and Billy and me jumping around in it while Mother sat on the sand. Sometimes we shared the beach with white-robed Cherubims and Seraphims, an African Christian sect that I thought of as strange, having nothing at all to do with us.

A door to a wider world opened to me just down the block from our apartment—the United States Information Service library, where I checked out life stories of George Washington and Thomas Jefferson. A Baptist girl in the States sent me a copy of *The Secret Garden*, and I read it in a snap. I read American magazines from mission coffee tables— *Ladies' Home Journal*, *McCall's*, *Reader's Digest*. I picked out an occasional novel for myself at Kingsway—English paperbacks, one about two girls whose identities were switched at birth in a hospital, another called *Ballet Shoes*, about three girls who were

Joseph Akinola, who accompanied us on our moves

born in different countries but grew up English together and learned to dance. Mother bought me an illustrated ballet book that showed the five basic positions, and an eleven-year-old English girl I met gave me a dance lesson. After Daddy told me I couldn't take ballet lessons when we went back to the States because dancing was un-Christian, Mother found me sniffling in the bathroom.

I loved movies just as much as books, maybe more. Now that we lived in Lagos and Ibadan instead of Iwo and Oyo, we could go to the "cinema"—*Show Boat, Robin Hood, Alice in Wonderland*. The movies were shown in open-air theatres with a moon sometimes floating above the tall screen. Most Nigerians sat in the flat unroofed area right in front of the screen while foreigners and Nigerians who could afford the higher price sat in raised seats higher up, below a roof for protection if it rained. Before the movie began, young uniformed Queen Elizabeth II appeared on screen seated high on a horse with the Union Jack waving and a band playing "God Save Our Gracious Queen." To this day, when Americans around me hear "My Country 'Tis of Thee," I hear "God save our gracious queen. . . ."

I was at that moment a subject of the queen, living in her empire, in one of the pink countries that dotted the globe we brought with us from the United States. Her face decorated the stamps I collected and stuck with bits of scotch tape into my stamp album. From my point of view in Nigeria in the mid-1950s, England was a world power while the United States was a backwater wannabe. I had no idea of the great political drama playing out right under my nose—the dissolution of the British Empire, symbolized by the movies that rivaled American films in popularity in Nigerian cinemas: products of free India. We never went to them, but from our apartment in Lagos I could hear their music from the cinema down the street: long plaintive ribbons of song strung out by female voices.

For me, those Lagos months were an idyllic time, but despite the ocean breeze, Billy still coughed, and then he came down again with what Mother took to be the amoebic dysentery she'd hoped he'd shaken. She gave him Milibis, though she feared it was toxic because it contained arsenic. He woke up and cried in the night. A few nights later he was so choked with asthma that Joseph ran for a taxi and we took Billy to the local hospital, where a doctor diagnosed pneumonia. He told Mother she would have to leave him overnight—and she could not stay with him. She refused, and the doctor made her sign a statement that she was taking Billy away against his orders—a moment so awful that she would recall it again and again for the rest of her life. She wrote Eleanor, "To tell the truth, I wonder what is going to happen to us."

The rains came and we returned to Ibadan, where I began having nightmares. I dreamed of monsters. One, a giant mechanical thing, stalked the land. Another slid under my door and loomed over my bed. Despite the lullaby of village drums that accompanied our nights, despite the watchman sleeping in the carport just outside my window, I was afraid to sleep in my room alone. I slept with Mother and Billy while Daddy moved to my bed. Puzzled, he wrote Eleanor, "We don't know the explanation for this but trust it will pass over." In one guilty dream, Jesus looked down on me from the cross and said, "You put me here." Riding along in the backseat of the car the next day, I leaned up against the front seat and told Daddy my dream. I thought he would be impressed: Jesus spoke to me! "I don't pay much attention to dreams," he said.

We were barely back in Ibadan when Billy stayed awake at nights coughing and wheezing. As the Harmattan approached again, the mission's executive committee advised Mother, Billy, and me to move back to Lagos. We were going to have to turn the press house over to other missionaries anyway—the three of us might as well move to Lagos where Billy could be better, if not well. Daddy would spend most of his time 120 miles from us in Ibadan. In the midst of this transition, we were heading for Lagos together in the rain when Daddy slowed for a lorry ahead of us, and the brakes grabbed. The car spun, plunged through a grassy field, rolled over, and came to rest on its side.

The lorry stopped and its passengers helped pull us out of the side windows of the car—alive and unhurt. I had been thrown under the dashboard instead of through the front window. Tall Joseph had escaped injury by leaning down to protect Billy. Mother, Billy, Joseph, and I caught a ride back to Ibadan, while passersby helped Daddy turn the car right side up, and he drove back to Ibadan to pick us up in our battered car. The car went into a shop and emerged looking like new, but mother wrote Eleanor, "I wonder if I will ever be able to relax in a car again." I don't believe she ever did.

✗ₒ

Our third residence in a single year was a small second-story flat on the Igbobi College compound in Yaba, on the edge of Lagos. Large lacy trees shaded sandy, spacious grounds. We all slept in one room and were not as close to the ocean as Mother and Daddy would have liked for Billy's sake, but this was the best place they could find in the time that they had, pressed as they were not only by the need to get Billy out of the Ibadan Harmattan and us out of the Ibadan house, but also by the demands of Daddy's work.

"Neville is under a terrible strain," Mother wrote Eleanor in late October 1954, not long after we moved. On top of directing the Training Union—his regular job—he was doing the work of the Nigerian Baptist Convention's Sunday School director while she was on furlough. Besides, there was extra mission travel unconnected with either job. The following week he was going with a committee to the Gold Coast to study the work there. Then, after four or five days back home, he would go to far eastern Nigeria with another committee to choose a house site for a new mission station.

His was a complex job description, and if this were an ordinary job and not a religious calling, I would be tempted to say that he was being exploited: asked to wear so many hats for such very low pay, and at a time when moving around and Billy's illness made further demands on his energy. But this was no ordinary job—it was a little like the U.S. military, which was moving my mother's sister, Polly, and her sergeant husband and children around other parts of the globe. Even the mission's terminology mirrored the military's: *furloughs*, *tours* (of duty), the very word *mission* itself.

Like military families, we lost the security of staying in one place but we gained something ordinary workers in the United States often lacked—guaranteed housing, transportation, and health care, which may not have been state-of-the-art but was, at least, available to us in a country where health care was scarce. In exchange for that security, we were locked into our lives. Missionaries did not often leave the field, although Mother had raised the possibility to Eleanor that, because of Billy's illness, the Board might not let us go back. She appeared to think that decision was the Board's, not hers and my father's, as if they themselves would not think of giving up their life's work for the sake of their son's health, as if once they became missionaries, they could imagine no other future for themselves.

I do not remember having any thoughts at all on the subject at the time—to me, this was our life and we were living it. As an adult, I *would* have bitter thoughts as I saw my brother deal with what I believe were the consequences of his prolonged illness. Why, I wondered, did our parents not simply take us all home to America? In fact, in her final years Mother told me that they did at one point try to stay home for Billy's sake—probably after this second tour—but Daddy could not find a church that would call him as pastor. Not until that moment had I considered that their mission work, however much it was a calling, was also a job. Daddy did later on get a job in the States for a while raising funds for a new Baptist college in Louisville while Billy was finishing high school, and Mother found a job for herself, too, teaching accounting and typing in a high school. I suspect the bottom-line reason they persevered in their work was less the lack of alternatives than the strength of their belief that they were "called" to be missionaries, Daddy especially, but Mother too because her life was so bonded with his.

Anyone blessed, or afflicted, with work they feel is specially theirs will know what I mean. God need not enter into it; it is enough to feel that here is work (medicine, farming, building a business, teaching, writing) that you were cut out to do, were meant to do, were born to do, work that gives your life meaning. My parents' faith provided something the rest of us don't always have: trust that God would see them through. The hymns they had sung growing up in the country and small town churches of early twentieth century mid-America held out a promise: "God will take care of you…" "Leaning on the everlasting arms…" and Daddy's favorite, "Lead kindly light, against the encircling gloom, lead thou me on." Following that kindly light, my father—the man who the Board psychiatrist said chose the hardest road—was not likely to give up, no matter how complicated our days. He stayed in a little apartment in the new Baptist Building in Ibadan and traveled back and forth to visit us in Yaba when he could. Mother told Eleanor that Daddy was always so tired. "We all are."

She was speaking for the adults. I loved our life on the Igbobi compound. I eased out of bed in the grey dawn light, tiptoed across the wooden floor through the kitchen, inched the screen door open, and slipped down the outside stairs into the dawning world. It was nearly cool at this time of day, and no one but me walked the dirt road through the compound past a gnarled tree with a pool of water held by a natural bowl in its thick trunk, its limbs still dark against the grey sky. I had roughly half a magic hour, each moment less magic than the one before as color seeped into the grey world.

Once Billy was awake, we could play together—he was four now, I was nine, not too far apart to play cowboys and Indians. If it was not too hot, we dressed up in cowboy outfits Aunt Eleanor sent, or else we just played Indians, although Mother said, "Carol Ann's problem now is how to be a squaw and a brave at the same time." For feathers she fixed leaves in my pigtails; since Billy's hair was so short she attached his feather to a string around his head. Now, she said, "he is a 'weal Indian.'"

We had other playmates, too. There was a Nigerian boy halfway in age between Billy and me who drifted in and out of our lives. He did not speak our language and we did not speak his, but we shared the common language of commerce. Whenever he showed up, we laid out bits of things we had scrounged and bought and sold to each other. We paid in hard red seeds that fell bountifully from the trees shading the compound. That our seed supply seemed unlimited did not affect its value as currency. British army children lived nearby, and we sometimes played with them. I became friends with one in particular—a girl with a British army father and an Indian mother.

Living on a compound without ties to the Baptist mission, Mother, Billy, and I were eddying out from the mission world. The piano teacher Mother took me to by taxi was the wife of a British army major, and we became special friends with an English couple, the Glennys, and an Irish family, the Luttons. Although Mother agreed with Daddy that the Glennys were "slightly anti-American (as most British folks are)," our relations with them and the Luttons, all fellow Baptists, were friendly, and grew closer as time went on. The Glennys took us every week to Victoria Beach where I surfed on a stubby surfboard rented from a line of boards stuck into the sand. The surf at Victoria Beach was hard, the undertow strong. People drowned there, but I was not afraid. I tucked the square end of the board into my skinny hip and waited for a wave, then at exactly the right moment before the wave hit, hurled myself down on the board and sped toward the shore till the board hit the sand with a bump and beached us both.

*

Nothing lasts, I already knew, and our Lagos life ended. In March 1955 Daddy needed to go to the Gold Coast and took us with him in the hope that the trip would lift Mother out of the deep fatigue in which she had fallen. We rode down a coastal road lined with coconut groves to Accra, where we stayed several days in an Assembly of God rest house not far from the beach. It was restful for Mother but it was not enough.

By April, back in Nigeria with Billy sick with asthma again and me feeling like a martyr if I had to work two hours a day on my schoolwork, Mother was herself spending two hours a day in bed, because, she wrote home in April, she just could not keep going. She and Daddy hoped the next furlough would give them a chance to rest, although Daddy planned to work on his thesis and there would of course be speaking engagements at churches. Family relations needed tending,

As a tourist in the northern city of Kano,
where I went to see an eye doctor

Stopping in the Swiss Alps on the way back to the United States

too. Daddy's sister Doris was struggling to raise her two boys after her husband died in a motorcycle accident; she had all but stopped writing us. Eleanor had moved off to teach in Troy, Ohio, and was thinking about moving to Florida, although Mother and Daddy hoped she would come back to Kentucky so they could see more of her while we were home.

For most of these seven years since we had first left Kentucky, we had been connected by a thread of words passing back and forth across the sea—a repeated reminder that we had not disappeared, that we were not gone for good, that we would one day return. And every three years we did return, bearing gifts: elephants carved out of ebony or birds of cow horns bought from Hausa traders who went from door to door on Europeans' compounds, spreading out their carvings and bronze and leather goods on our front porches. This time, Mother told Eleanor, we were sending home, at considerable expense, a box of mahogany elephant coffee tables.

Months before we left, Mother started figuring out what clothes we could put together to wear on the trip home through Europe: my old red jacket for Billy, for me, an old corduroy coat another girl outgrew. We planned sightseeing stops in Amsterdam, Zurich, and Rome, and then London, where we would visit the ladies we'd stayed with before. Mother and Daddy were also making plans for our furlough. They hoped to buy a house in Louisville, where Daddy would go on working on his doctorate at the seminary. Mother and Daddy would put the $100-a-month rent money from the board into house payments and then after we left, rent the house out in order to pay the mortgage. They did not know how they would pay for furnishing the house, but Daddy still hoped he could scrounge the cash to buy a new car in New York and drive for a year in style before he sold it.

During our furlough year in Louisville, we did not, after all, buy a new car—we bought an old one. We did buy a house, though, and it was old, too, with a crumbling wooden porch that we replaced with concrete. I went to George Rogers Clark again and found classmates I'd known in second grade still there in the sixth. I sang in the Louisville Children's Chorus and rode to rehearsals with other girls, on one such trip embarrassing myself by not knowing the name of the vice president of the United States. There was no talk of leaving me "home" in America, though in a scrap of autobiography I would write for the new missionary kids' school that was about to open in Nigeria, I said this year was the happiest in my life because I had friends and so much to do, and was, besides, baptized, made officially Christian and Southern Baptist.

On trips to Kentucky churches where my parents spoke about missions, we were treated like visiting royalty from a foreign land, and I felt, in my frilly new dress and black patent leather shoes, as if I really was: a regular princess in these country churches where frazzled women fanned themselves with funeral-home fans. However I might appear to the faithful, I was a secular girl. I sang "Que Sera" with Doris Day, "The Wayward Wind" with Gogi Grant. Yul Brynner waltzed Deborah Kerr across the floor in *The King and I*, and something melted inside of me.

We started back to Africa on August 14, 1956, on an American ship with officers who wore white dress uniforms to dinner and a first mate who let me pick the movie we would watch one more time. I liked *Lili* best—a young awkward girl dancing herself into womanhood. The screen, hung on a mast, rose and fell with the rolling ship, and above the sea, the sky was full of stars.

We stopped in Monrovia, where balconies hung from greyed wooden houses and I could buy comics with limp dollar bills. Then the ship bypassed Nigeria and journeyed on down the coast to the Congo River, which we floated up after dark, guided by new red and green lights flashing on and off for miles, to the port of Boma, then back to the Atlantic and down the coast to Angola, then up the coast again for a stop in French Cameroons. After a month on board, we arrived in Lagos. Walking down the dock, I felt watched by the workers we passed, and new feelings stirred.

The dorm at Newton Memorial School, the boarding school for MKs
(photo by Wilfred Congdon)

Swept Away

Once a child who spilled out everything she did and thought, I was now a girl who had secrets. When we visited the Oshogbo compound where the mission had built the new boarding school for MKs, I Indian-wrestled with a boy on the grass and, his face inches from mine, felt a wave of something I had never felt before. It was such a strange feeling that, in the car going home, I came close to leaning forward from the back seat and telling my parents about it—but instead sat still and kept this discovery, of whatever it was, deliciously to myself.

If Mother and Daddy noticed a change in me, they did not let on in their letters home, which they wrote less often now because they were more overwhelmed than ever by all they had to do. On top of the Training Union work, they were operating what amounted to a bed and breakfast for the stream of colleagues who traveled to Ibadan to shop or conduct mission business. And because the house was new, they were supervising grass planting, furniture making, and electrical installation. Daddy himself laid new tile he hoped would contain the dust from the concrete and keep Billy's asthma at bay.

They were doing all this settling in while not knowing for sure if we would go on living in Ibadan. We were no sooner off the boat in Lagos when we heard the news that Daddy's office might be moved to Ilorin, about 100 miles north of Ibadan. As Mother told the tale to the folks back home, some missionaries resented the power wielded by missionaries stationed in Ibadan and wanted to break it up by scattering administrative offices around. "We just hope the Lord is in it," she said. "We are for it if it is for the advancement of the work, even though it means personal disruption, etc. We are going to try not to think too much about it."

The Nigerian-controlled Baptist Convention would vote on the move the next April. That meant several months of uncertainty. This prospect of yet another move could not have improved Mother's spirits. Further unsettling her peace of mind, there was the possibility that I might leave home to attend the new MK boarding school. It was nearly a two-hour drive from Ibadan, and I would get home only one weekend a month. One day I wanted to go, the next day I didn't. "If she wants to go," Mother wrote her brother Harry in Memphis, "I guess we will let her."

What passed through my eleven-year-old thoughts as I weighed trading in my family for kids my own age? I had spent almost every day of my life with one or both of my parents and, after he was born, with my brother. Yet if I went on living at home in Ibadan, I would go on not having friends my own age. Ann Eaglesfield was still in Ibadan but lived across town.

For my twelfth birthday in February I was hoping to have a slumber party—except who else would I invite?

For me, the memorable event of a March 1957 trip to Ghana (the name the Gold Coast had just taken on independence from British rule) was not seeing Elmina Castle where so many slaves had passed through, it was walking with a twelve-year-old MK boy on a pipeline across a lagoon. On a trip to the watery East where heavy rains drummed hard on tin roofs, I played with Mary Katherine Howell, who was from Texas and had nicer clothes than I did and gave some of them to me. Then I was back in Ibadan, and once more mostly alone.

In the end, we postponed the decision about boarding school, and I went through seventh grade at home in Ibadan, where mission headquarters stayed after all. Billy and I played jacks, pickup sticks, and endless games of Monopoly. Or I took off on my own, exploring the farms behind the house—strolling with my hiking stick through rows of cassava, occasionally meeting and greeting a farmer strolling along, too, with a gun over his shoulder to shoot an aparo if one happened by.

But most days I settled down with a book into my reading chair, a chaise lounge Mother had covered in a blue print fabric that matched the skirt she made for my dressing table. As I read, I sipped a Coca-Cola and nibbled a cucumber until lunchtime, when I brought my book to the table and kept right on reading. I read my way through the books on my bedroom shelves, and then I read them again. In lieu of flesh-and-blood companions, I had Pollyanna, the Sugar

Fishermen on the coast of Ghana

With Billy at Elmina Castle

Creek Gang, and Anne of Green Gables, who like me read a lot and saw life through a rose-colored imagination. Then, in a flash one September day in 1957, this life I was used to living was over.

✂

Our new apple-green Chevrolet had barely disappeared down the drive at Newton Memorial School when an ache of homesickness slid into my throat—and a current of other children swept me away: Roger and Richard and Johnny from Iwo, Gita from Shaki, Jim Pool from Ogbomosho. As more and more arrived, the dormitory pulsed with the energy of our coming together. Two younger boys caught the wave, burst out in cries of "Cheer!" "Despair!" "Grief!" "Joy!" Soon we were all doing it, like evangelicals seized by the spirit.

Our teachers and houseparents (Aunt Esther and Uncle Wilfred Congdon from Iwo days) packed our days with activities from one end to the other. After breakfast, boys carried girls' books down to the two classrooms where teachers kept us on task while we went on using correspondence courses just like we did at home: Calvert for grades four through eight, University of Nebraska High School Extension once we moved into ninth grade. After lunch, a rest period on our bunkbeds, more studying, and then exuberant sports: pole vaulting on the lawn or Capture the Flag under the trees or baseball in the field behind the dormitory.

I could do it all, more or less, though for baseball I was sent to center field where I could do the least damage.

If a high ball hurtled my way out of the sky, I froze in fear. Since my strabismus prevented me from seeing in depth, the ball coming at me could be a few inches to either the right or the left depending on which eye I used to see it—not a chance I would catch it. I was better at tennis with the ball skimming over the net, and I liked tennis better, too, because it gave me time alone with my boyfriend of the week, especially Jonathan Low, his teenage dogtag flashing against his tanned skin as he loped across the court. In the States, teen boys gave their dogtags to their girlfriends. I could hope.

In the evenings, we had devotionals and homework, but we had parties, too: for Valentine's, Halloween, birthdays. Girls rolled their hair up on rollers the night before and wore their best dresses with full skirts puffing out over stiff half-slips. Boys wore suits and ties and flipped their hair in front like Elvis Presley.

All the adults on the compound helped organize things, but the top organizer around was the grandmother of one of the younger boys, a retired teacher from Iowa who put us through the paces of wholesome activities for the young. We memorized poems ("The highwayman came riding, riding riding..."), put on plays, voted each other into office in Girls' Auxiliary and Royal Ambassadors (Baptist alternatives to Girl Scouts and Boy Scouts), Training Union, citizens' club. We held debates: "Resolved: that women are qualified to be president" and, in this time when Ghana was already independent and Nigeria was about to be, "Resolved: Africa is ready for independence." We might talk about Africa, but we were learning to be Americans. We listened to the World Series broadcast by the Voice of America through static we were told was the Russians

Newton students with housemother Esther Congdon (top, second from right) in a photo taken by housefather Wilfred Congdon

Playing music in the Newton living room
(used with permission: Charles L. Gillespie, IMB, SBC)

jamming the signal, and all proclaimed ourselves Dodgers or Yankees. On the night the VOA announced the Russian satellite Sputnik was coming over, we went outside to search the starry sky for a moving point of light.

Newton was like a livelier mission meeting, that one time of the year when we had lots of other kids to play with—except for a big difference: at mission meeting, we were a sideshow, keeping ourselves entertained while adults did the real work. Here, at Newton, we were doing real work, cheered on by a half dozen adults whose job was to help us learn—not only algebra and Latin but also how to be responsible members of a community, an American community.

There would be a downside to all this: the high school world we would return to in the United States would not knock itself out for us in the way the adults at Newton did. Back in the States, we would no longer be the center of attention—no longer the stars of our MK show. We would in fact be odd ducks, plunged into an American teen world clutching shards of teenage life we had scraped together in Nigeria: Ricky Nelson singing "Big Man" on a 45 record that Jonathan brought back from the States or a teen magazine with its story of young drivers playing "Chicken" on the highway. While American teenagers were necking in cars at drive-ins, we were flashing messages between the boys' and girls' wings from atop the storage shelves in our dorm rooms after Uncle Wilfred played "Taps" to signal lights out. While Americans teens watched Troy Donahue and Sandra Dee kiss in *A Summer Place*, we watched black-and-white Mickey Mouse cartoons or documentaries about national parks.

Tame as our teenage life was, it was full to the brim. Reporting the news to my family, I ratcheted along like an old-fashioned radio newscaster. Reading my letters now I hardly recognize the girl writing them. The Newton self I remember played "Blue Moon" in the piano room, held hands with a boy on movie nights, felt his finger trail up her wrist: a dreamy girl, except on the tennis court or down in a ditch during a game of Capture the Flag, and even then a girl self-contained. This girl of the letters was as jittery as a Junebug, on stage every minute. I wrote Aunt Eleanor after one Girls' Auxiliary coronation: "Four maidens were recognized and five queens were crowned. I'm happy to say I was one of the queens! I wore my new green net evening dress, my new patent leather shoes, and my new bracelet you sent me. I was really proud of it, and it matched the earrings I wore which were each a single cut-glass stone which glittered different colors."

Who *is* that girl? She wears me out—what an act she puts on! The girl I remember from my three years at Newton was quieter, sometimes a little low in spirits. Perplexed by the dissonance between memory and the letters as I read them decades later, I turned to my old friend Gerald Coomer one spring afternoon on a bench at Spring Mill, a pioneer village in Indiana. Gerald knows me well: I can say anything to him at any length and he will listen, and that afternoon he did, as I poured out my Newton memories. He asked questions, led me along until, suddenly, I was moved nearly to tears by the kind of sudden knowing that spills out in a psychiatrist's office: however much fun I had at Newton, our Newton life shook me to the core, leaving behind, beneath the tumult of memories, a residue of sadness.

I who up to that time had ordered my days pretty much as I pleased, at Newton lost control. I who had spent hours roaming freely in my own imagination, at Newton followed a pattern fixed by other people. To the confusion of being twelve, I who had been nearly alone became at Newton one of many. An image flashes through my mind: curled up in a ball, my arms wrapped around my knees, making myself small while around me children flailed their arms, jumped up and down, yelled, "Cheer!" "Joy!" "Despair!" I was a little boat swept along in a current nearly too fast for me to handle.

*

After my first five months at Newton, I was talking about not going back the next year for ninth grade. Mother knew Billy would like that. "He has missed Carol Ann so much," she wrote Eleanor, "and said before she came home he'd forgotten what she looked like." Mother and Daddy would be glad to have me home, too, but Mother thought all these activities were good for me, "besides the fellowship and learning to get along with others." There was, however, another possibility: that a school for American children might open in Ibadan. Then I could stay home and go there, and so could Billy, who was not yet old enough to go to Newton, and, besides, still had worrisome bouts with asthma.

But my parents were shorter than ever of funds. Mother and Daddy had borrowed $150 from Aunt Eleanor when we returned to Nigeria in October 1956. A year later, Daddy was buying petrol by the gallon and borrowing from Billy's allowance to pay for that. The cost of living was rising and their salaries remained the same. The washing machine went bad and so did the sewing machine. Mother thought of asking me to help her buy a new one with my savings from my allowance; it would then be considered "mine." A friend who was supervising the two rental apartments in our Louisville house wrote that both the house and its furniture were slowly falling to pieces. Mother talked about the possibility of getting a second mortgage.

In mid-February 1958, when Daddy stopped to see me at Newton, for a moment I did not recognize this man walking past the classroom windows, his shoulders slumped: my Daddy. Carl Whirley had told Mother a few months earlier that when he saw him at the Baptist Convention, Daddy, then forty-two, looked "old and haggard." And here he was off on a six-week journey North with hours of hard driving through swirls of dust over untarred roads, accompanied by Mr. Bamikole, who had been his associate now for eight years. While Mr. Bamikole stayed in Yoruba homes, Daddy stayed with other missionaries or in rest houses or slept on a cot in a church or classroom building. Of his night at one government rest house, he wrote,

> There was no water handy, no tables, nor chairs, nothing in the room, I put up my cot, ate a tin of pork and beans, drank an orange crush (new drink made at Kano) and went to the meeting where I waited for about 40 minutes for the few people who

turned up. At 9, I went back to get my supper—almost too tired to do so but you know me—I had to eat. I set my stove on the floor, washed my dishes on the camp cot, sat and ate on the cot also. In other words, my bed became almost everything to me. Except for the Moslem next door having his 11 p.m. prayers with all the chants I slept well through the night.

Sometimes it was so hot he had trouble sleeping and sat in his underwear to type out his letters, which were punctuated with tire trouble and car repairs.

Whatever hardships he experienced were nothing compared to that of the five missionaries he was reading about in a book called *Through Gates of Splendor*: they had been killed on their first visit to an indigenous community in Amazonian Ecuador. "Their faith seems to put our own to shame," he wrote Mother. "However, I am sure that much of the work we are doing will count as much for the Glory of Christ. I certainly do not feel like a martyr in my work, but I feel definitely and loyally committed to it, and I do not believe that even in a land like Nigeria, where there is some law and order, the work is certainly not all easy to the point of being luxury."

There was in fact a break in Nigerian law and order while he was on the road. Riots erupted in Ibadan after a political leader was killed in a car accident and some of his supporters blamed a rival leader. There were times when Mother, Billy, and Ethel Harmon, the single woman missionary who ran the Nigerian Sunday School program, were the only ones left on our Ibadan compound, and Aunt Ethel told Mother she could hardly sleep at night.

Meanwhile, work went on: Mother was typing and editing Yoruba lessons for adults and children and delivering them to the Baptist Press. In his letters Daddy thanked her for helping with what he tellingly referred to as *his* work. He told her he missed her and loved her. At one point he opened and shut a door to a possibility I knew nothing about: that after their furlough he might return to Nigeria with Mother staying home in the States—I suppose either because of Billy's health or to see me through high school. "I don't want to live here without you," he said. When Mother told him about some unpleasantness she'd encountered from one of the other missionaries, he replied, "Just forget her—I'll take care of her when I get home. Her troubling my little wife."

※

While Daddy traveled the roads of the North, Africa receded from view in my life at boarding school. Gone were our family stops along Ibadan streets to buy bread from women who ran with their loaves to the car or a beancake called akara or a long crispy concoction we called antelope horns, fried in a roadside pan over a charcoal fire. At home, Joseph still practically lived in our midst; he had a little house behind ours where he stayed sometimes, especially when Daddy was away. I can't even remember the names of household staff at Newton, while I can still feel Joseph's arms around me in a welcoming hug when I came home from school—until the day Mother and Daddy said

I was getting too old for that. Sniffing discrimination in the air, I asked if that meant I was too old to hug Dr. Patterson, head of the mission and a grandfatherly figure. Well, of course, not. So there, I thought: I see how things are.

Just how nervous did missionary parents feel as their children reached their teen years? Even when I was very young, young men would call out to me, "Be my wife! Be my wife!" and offer Daddy a respectable number of cows for me. I always assumed they were teasing, but I suspect one of my fellow MKs was right when she suggested that missionaries used to leave their children at home before their teens to forestall intimate relations between their offspring and Africa's.

At Newton, MKs courted under the watchful eyes of our adult chaperones: boys bought girls Coca-Colas, carried their books, wrote notes folded up in tiny squares and passed through trusted friends. I have a fat envelope of them still and am struck by how sweet they were, how thoughtful we seemed: assuring each other of our friendship, exchanging gifts, compliments, even moral instruction. When I left Jonathan behind for someone else, he wrote, "Would you not keep changing around? It doesn't make boys feel good when girls treat them that way."

Close to each other, we were all the more distant from the Nigerian city of Oshogbo, just down the road. We did attend Sunday worship services in churches in town, and in mid-May 1958, we visited the head gardener's house so the boys could meet a requirement to advance up the Royal Ambassador ranks. I wrote Mother and Daddy, "Sunday afternoon all of us kids except Gita, Alice Anne, and Mary Margaret went to Baba Shegun's house. He's the head gardener. We sang hymns

Taking a lorry to church service in Oshogbo

Our rope swing near the Newton dormitory

and some of the boys played their instruments. It was for the R.A.'s 'knightly deed' and we girls went along for fun. We sat in a circle and about 50 Africans crowded around us. Everything from whooping cough to leprosy was in that crowd."

I wonder what diverse meanings that last sentence holds. It was on the one hand a comment from a girl who had had malaria half a dozen times by the age of eleven, watched her brother struggle for breath year after year, suffered a stream of immunizations against small pox, yellow fever, tetanus, and typhoid, and visited "leper colonies" at an early age. Waves of sickness swept through Newton—measles, malaria, and unidentified maladies. I grew up knowing not to drink water that had not been boiled or filtered and not to eat food from street vendors unless it came right out of a pot over a fire. This was the tropics, close to the equator, prime climate for proliferating bacteria. Public health and sanitation systems were nearly nonexistent. Missionaries and their children got ill often enough. One three-year-old missionary child in Ghana died while I was at Newton. He came in from playing, said he couldn't see, and, possibly victim of a snakebite, fell down dead.

So you might charitably say that I was accurately assessing conditions I had learned to be careful of. You might also wonder if I wanted to send a frisson of fear through my mother, who, when she heard about an all-day hike we took through the heat of the day, hit the ceiling. Or you could read those last two sentences as a fair assessment of how *other* those "50 Africans crowded around us" were to me in my thirteenth year.

ϗ

With eighth grade nearly over, Mother told our housemother, Esther Congdon, that she would like for me to stay home and go with Billy to the new Ibadan school the next year. Mother had been the only teacher Billy had had since kindergarten, and she thought he desperately needed classroom experience. He and I could both go to the school for just a little more than the $400 cost of sending me to Newton for the year. But there would be only one teacher for several grades in the new school, and the month had not yet ended when she abandoned the idea. I would, after all, go back to Newton in the fall of 1958—as the mission stepped quietly into the stream of American history.

While angry crowds tried to keep black children out of white schools in the American South in the wake of the Brown v. Board of Education decision, Newton (under a new policy admitting non-mission children preparing for higher education in the United States) welcomed Doy Sands, the daughter of an African-American family working in Ibadan. Her family and mine were friends, and Mother wrote home, "We are all happy that she is going. She is cute as can be. Carol Ann said she would not know she was even different if we did not discuss it! She has been in my Sunday School class a long time."

I *was* annoyed that they make such a big deal of it. Now a critical adolescent, I was quick to sniff out the smallest hint of racial prejudice or condescension. While I was feeling self-righteous, Mother was in fact busy launching her own private campaign for desegregation. In letters to family in the States, she mentioned a trip to Oshogbo, when a Nigerian pastor stayed with us in our mission quarters; she mentioned a Negro

Daddy visiting me at Newton

*Older students at Newton: (l. to r.) front row: John Whirley, Jarry
Richardson, Doy Sands, me, Linda Goldie; back row: Pat Hill,
Jonathan Low, Gita Richardson, Mary Katherine Howell*

American doctor and his wife from Tuskegee who had visited us; she mentioned her friendship with a young girl from the Cameroons who came to her "inquirer's class" but also came for lunch.

In their 1958 Christmas letter addressed to American friends and congregations that sent us money, cards, and gifts, Mother and Daddy laid out a panorama of our multicultural lives. While I was home for a weekend, they wrote, "we had two Florida A & M students (Negro) for lunch, along with Carol's piano teacher (a young Nigerian man in the music division of Nigerian Broadcasting Corporation) . . . . It was a real treat to get to see the A & M players in three American comedies that night." The new Baptist Chapel where Daddy was preaching in English was "truly an international house of worship with Americans (Negro and white), Canadians, Swiss, English, Irish, German, and Lebanese, and various African tribes attending. . . . . We have had in our home American business and professional peoples (Negro and white), American students, and Irish, English, German, and African friends. So if we, along with our children, do not see the world as the field, it will be our own fault."

Years later when I realized how a lot of church folks in the States would respond to all this social mixing in 1958, I would understand that my parents were speaking up, in their own way, for desegregation. If they were responding in part to the American civil rights movement, they were also responding to Africa's changing times. The Gold Coast had become independent Ghana the year before. Nigeria would be independent in two years. Resistance to apartheid in South

Africa was rising. Alan Paton, the white South African novelist who wrote *Cry, the Beloved Country,* spoke at the Baptist Chapel in Ibadan where Daddy was pastor. "He surely has done some wonderful writing," Mother wrote Eleanor, "and his speaking reflects the same love and concern for the people of S. Africa."

Five years down the road, after a church bombing killed four young girls in Birmingham, Alabama, my father would write to both Governor George Wallace and President John F. Kennedy, asking them to do their part to "bring about peaceful integration." He also wrote to the Foreign Mission Board's secretary for Africa expressing his concern about the impact events in the South were having on mission work. And he wrote his friend Carl Whirley on furlough in Birmingham that he was discomfited, "as were others, by the statement in *Time* magazine to the effect that if Southern Baptists would take hold of this civil rights problem and do something tangible about it the whole situation in the South could be changed. This did not particularly make me happy and proud to be called a Southern Baptist." In their letters of 1958, my parents seemed already to be taking their own stand, hoping to preach by example—to provide evidence from their own lives that blacks and whites could come together in peaceful fellowship, even, as one picture of Daddy presiding at a chapel wedding attests, in marriage.

Mother's relations with the most important black man in my life—Joseph—were not, however, so peaceful. One day she said she thought she would just sack him—he was not cleaning things well and hadn't cleaned under the sink when she asked him to. Billy went into the kitchen and told Joseph he would help him clean, and he did. But there was already too much water under the bridge— "too much palaver," said Mother. In late April, she wrote Eleanor, "We let Joseph go finally. After all these years."

Not long after he left, Joseph visited the house with his children, bringing sugar cane for Billy and me and limes for Mother—maybe a peace offering with the hope of coming back, maybe just a peace offering. Maybe he was tired of the palaver, too, and the heavy workload. But surely he missed us, and we missed him. He had been there for us all those times when my father was not— an intimate part of our life, waiting for us when we came back from trips, sweeping us up in his strong arms. Now, in a flash, he was gone. I can see him now, his deep brown handsome face, his broad smile—my everlasting image of what a man should be.

Whatever Mother felt about firing Joseph, his departure had consequences for her. She thought she might be able to manage alone if she just didn't have so much company—missionaries streaming in to Ibadan on business of one sort or another. That's what she told Eleanor, and in the next breath said the lights were off "and you should see the dishes! Haven't washed any today. And no ironing done—the refrigerator dripping. One day we have no lights, the next no water." Daddy had promised to install the water filter they'd had for over a year but hadn't, so she boiled water for drinking.

While Mother was boiling water in Ibadan, I was too caught up in my own swirl of activity to miss Joseph. The competitive spirit at Newton kept my head swimming. Who played the piano best? Ping-pong? Tennis? Had the biggest stamp collection? Ran fastest? Who would be chosen Valentine king and queen? I played the piano well, but I wished I were motherly like Gita Richardson, who was better with babies. I had long blonde hair, but Linda Goldie had curves where I didn't. I could play tennis with boys, but Mary Katherine Howell could surge ahead in a foot race, head held high, skirt and red petticoat churning, gliding first across the finish line. I would even have liked having the *je ne sais quoi* of Alice Anne Burks, who came late to the mission field and retained something exotic—the American normal.

I was devastated when I failed, as I failed so miserably one night during the evening devotional. I had long been a performer, playing piano for guests and services at the Ibadan chapel, but what I wanted to do most of all was sing. I had never had voice lessons, but I had sung in the children's chorus in Louisville on our last furlough, and I wanted more than anything to be Shirley Jones on a Broadway stage, rich voice soaring: "When you walk through a storm, hold your head up high."

But that night when I set off through a hymn solo, an awful thickness in my throat choked the tune into silence.

I fared better at the Girls' Auxiliary coronation when I received my gold-painted wooden scepter and, without stumbling, testified to my faith: "In my heart there is the warm feeling of knowing that if ever I am lonely, or sad, or in trouble, I can turn to the Great Comforter in prayer. I am only a child in Christ, but I hope that some day, I too will walk continuously with Jesus, and live every hour of the day for my God."

How did that pious girl turn just a few years later into a woman on a decidedly more worldly trajectory? Our Newton newspaper offers a clue: a story I wrote for English class, "The House of Mystery." A narrator riding through the rain on a summer night sees an old mansion with iron gates. She dismounts and lifts the knocker; the house comes alive with voices and tinkling music. Rain-soaked and bedraggled, she joins the party—fashionably dressed people, paper caps, colored streamers. She is offered "a glass of pale liquid with a slight tint of color in it." She takes a sip, the sensation pleases. She continues to indulge "this delightful new drink" and falls into a stupor . . . . She opens her eyes; her head aches; she feels queer all over. The sun is slipping up from the mountains to preside over another new day. Behind her there is no trace of the mysterious house, no clue to the night's adventure . . . . except for a piece of crepe paper streaming from her arm.

Long before my parents let me loose in America, I knew there are many ways to live and thoughts to think. I had been reading at a breakneck pace ever since I arrived at Newton. Even with plenty else to entertain me, shortly into my Newton life I had already read nine books in less than a month. Titles poured through my letters—Grace Livingston Hill's Christian romances, yes, but also *Pride and Prejudice*, *The Yearling*. On holiday in Ibadan, I read *The Bridge Over the River Kwai* and entered the mind of a man about to take another man's life. I sat on our front porch as the red sun went down behind the palm trees and read Thomas Wolfe's *Look Homeward, Angel* in a state of wonder that the world had such words in it: "O lost, and by the wind grieved, ghost, come back again."

I wriggled down under the covers of my bed at night and read *For Whom the Bell Tolls* with a flashlight. I knew my parents would not approve of whatever Robert and Maria were doing under their blanket in the hills of Spain. On a birthday boat ride to Tarqua Bay, I read a paperback of *Peyton Place* in plain view of Mother, Daddy, Billy, and the oarsman poling us across the harbor. Daddy caught a glimpse of the blurbs on the back cover and, suspicious, asked. "Carol Ann, is this something you should be reading?"

"Oh Daddy," said I, already wise beyond my years. "You know how publishers are—they just have to sell the book."

I read no books by Nigerian writers, who had barely started to publish fiction. I would not read Chinua Achebe's *Things Fall Apart*, published in 1958, until college. Except for a *Reader's Digest* condensed version of Alan Paton's *Too Late the Phalarope*, Africa had no place in my literary life, as it had had not much of a place in the rest of my life at Newton, where we were being put through the paces of learning to be American before it was too late and we found ourselves in high school in Birmingham or Louisville or, worse, with an aunt and uncle out in some little southern town where we would really be lost.

That time seemed to be approaching for me, but not as fast as I thought it was. When I moved back to Ibadan for the summer of 1959, this tour had already lasted the usual three years, but Mother and Daddy had decided to stay one more year, partly so they could be with me longer. They had thought hard about the decision, prayed over it, I am sure. Mother had once told Eleanor she'd like to stay in the States on their next furlough until I finished high school, but knew she couldn't do it unless it was God's will, "and that I will know when the time comes." Staying in Nigeria another year would delay the hour of decision.

That summer in Ibadan, I spent most of my time reading while Mother coped with the rounds of guests. One day we had eleven for lunch, nine for supper and breakfast. One week she washed sixteen sheets and forty-two napkins. She planned a birthday picnic for John Whirley but it rained all day so we had the party inside, played games, read comics, munched popcorn, and made messes that Mother cleaned up.

Finally she hired a new steward but still found herself doing most of the work. On top of maintaining the house, garden, and fenced yard where we kept the chickens that churches gave to Daddy until we ate them, we now had a horse: Sweetpea, the polo pony the Richardsons left for us when they went on furlough. Injuries had retired him from polo, but you could never tell it. He was frisky and ornery. He kicked you when you tried to mount or carried you into the garage and tried to hang you on the clotheslines. Tied up to eat grass, he broke loose and raced across the yard. We got him mainly for Billy, who had been excruciatingly lonely in the last year, but I, too, felt some sense of possession. "In the three days I've been here," I wrote Gita, "I've learned how to saddle him, ride him (to a certain extent), lead him, cut grass for him, carry his water, etc."

Billy and Sweetpea

In other news, I told Gita that I had taken charge of the children's Training Union Sunday night. I reported a conversation I'd had with one of the younger missionary children there:

He – Are all people human beings?
Me – Yes, people and human beings mean the same thing.
He– Are Africans human beings?
Me – Yes, everyone who can think, and talk, and read and write are human beings.
He – Oh.

I also wrote to Jonathan Low, who had written me expressing his concern about Roger's return from furlough and its possible effect on our relationship.

Dearest Jonathan,
Thanks for your note, but there's no reason why you should be afraid of Roger's coming. I am looking forward to it, but I'm also looking forward to Jim's, Alice Anne's, and Michael's arrival. Now, I am only interested in Roger as an older M.K. off the field, and I don't know how it will be when he gets back. If you're afraid I'll like him best when he gets back, please don't be. I'm not saying I won't, but remember that in a year a lot of things can happen. Next year there will probably be several changes during the year, and I don't usually like the same

boy all year. I haven't this year. Does that answer your question? You know, I have as much cause to be afraid you'll like Alice Anne as you have to be afraid I'll like Roger. Don't worry about next year till it comes. After all, I think there'll be a pretty even number of boys & girls!

I like you now, and I may like you next year, but I'm no prophet, neither are you, so don't try to be! Are you mad at me now? Please don't be.

Very sincerely yours,

Ca.

My relationship the next year with another boy turned out to be my most daring at Newton. On steamy afternoons we retreated to the only private space we could find on the compound, a rough track cut through the bush where we stared at the purple morning glories while he wrapped his arms demurely around me. Daddy said if he found out I ever kissed a boy at Newton, he would bring me home, so we never kissed, but on a trip back from seeing a 1920s musical called *Lilac Time* in Ibadan, we cuddled in the back seat of the station wagon.

Sex was so off limits that no one—certainly not my parents—talked to me about it. One of the girls came up with a book on marriage that explained how women became pregnant—something along the lines of "in the closeness of the marriage bed the man's sperm unites with the egg." On a stay in Lagos my father and I shared a large bed in the hostel, never touching. Until my next period came, I worried: would

I become pregnant by my own father because we had slept in the same bed? Not until I went off to college and two girls on my freshman hall demonstrated the moves people make when they make love did I understand with any specificity just how the sperm found the egg.

✖

It was my last year at Newton—tenth grade—and we had new houseparents, very young—a father with dark curly hair, a red-headed mother with a ponytail that bounced when she walked, two small children, and, given the responsibility laid on her youthful shoulders, an understandably short fuse. After she cut off our Coca-Cola supply because a couple of kids said the price was too high, I complained in a letter home, and I also complained that we had to write our letters in the dining room on Saturday afternoon under her supervision.

"I can think of other things to say besides what she tells us!" I thought of plenty to say, reporting, for instance, that we now had to spend two hours a week on chores, which meant we had to cut out other things—for instance, piano practice, reduced to two hours a week on Saturday, maybe, depending on what else was going on. During rest period I read for thirty minutes and wrote letters for thirty minutes. That left no time for our Girls' Auxiliary work, I said. "What should we do?"

I was working hard to finish my courses by the end of school and pass my requirements for Queen Regent, which would add a green cape to the Girls' Auxiliary crown and

Girls' Auxiliary coronation, Newton 1960,
from Maidens to Queen Regent (me)

scepter I already had. I learned the names of Baptist home missionaries and embroidered a map of the world. I was feeling the strain. "I wish I could come home to Ibadan Saturday as I feel homesick—especially for some quiet. There's so much to do here I always feel rushed." I had a cough that came and went. Still, I played tennis. I wrote Mother I would be school champion if it were not for Pat Hill (though Jonathan had defeated me six to four that very morning).

The stress I felt that final year had a new dimension. I was more aware than ever of mission eyes watching: adults judging me, even off the Newton compound. The mission had always been like a small town where you could not escape the character assigned to you by the collective. From an early age we had all been characters on the mission stage. No one wanted to be the mission child pegged as a problem. I could not complain too much about the part I was set to play at Newton—the smart one, apparently, and I had an award from the University of Nebraska high school extension division to prove it.

But budding prima donna that I was, I resented any judgment. One remark I'd heard an adult had made about me sent me into a funk: I sat on the bathroom floor and sulked. Daddy once wrote Mother, "I surely would like to see the day come when each missionary would tend to his own business and stop talking about what others do and don't do." By this time, that's the way I felt, too. But I would soon be rid of the mission audience, released from the mission web. Soon I would be gone from Newton, from the mission, from Africa, and I was glad of it. I wrote Mother that I longed to be back in America.

I had already picked out the cities I wanted to visit on the way: Barcelona, Geneva, Frankfurt, Paris, London. I looked them up in the *Encyclopedia Britannica* to figure out what we would see in each place. Daddy wanted to go to Rio de Janeiro for the Baptist World Congress, and Mother and Billy and I would travel through Europe by ourselves. Eleanor wrote that if she were Daddy, she would not leave her family to go through Europe alone. "She just doesn't know how capable we are, does she?" said I.

I sent Mother a list of what I needed for our trip home: a white sweater set, three bras, a suit, a hat, underpants. I hoped Aunt Eleanor would send me loafers; I wore size 7. "Do you have any gloves I can wear? If not, I think I'll need some as the ones I've had here have one coffee stain, and one is missing. Can you get stockings out here? I think it would be nice to have a couple of pairs to wear occasionally on the way home." What about a straight skirt as well as the suit? And I only had one suitable nylon blouse, which might be too little by then—so what about a white blouse? I supplied my measurements (bust "31 ½"; hips "34," waist "23," shoulder to waist "16"). Mother thought I'd become clothes-conscious. I see me struggling out of the cocoon of childhood, trying to costume myself as an American woman.

The years at the Newton—and maybe the stream of letters in which I defined my self and life—had empowered me. I spoke up about one matter especially important to me: where we would live once we got back to the States. We owned the house in Louisville but it might already be rented out. My parents considered living in Frankfort because it seemed likely

I would stay there with Aunt Eleanor for my senior year in high school. I had a different idea. "I hope we live in Louisville because I feel that in a big school I'll have a better chance of finding someone who believes as I do about things," I said, already with an inkling of the rocky road ahead. Besides, I wrote, "I think of Louisville as my home."

I was to get what I wanted—Louisville—but, in the end, for the same reason that had dictated other places we had lived throughout our lives in Nigeria: the needs of the mission. "I guess you'd better sit down before you read the rest of this," Mother wrote Eleanor just a few months before we were to leave Nigeria. "Guess what? We are expecting an increase in our family! Not just one, not just twins, but possibly as many as six!" The mission board had decided to offer missionaries an MK "home" in Louisville for teenage children left behind by their parents, and my parents had been asked to run it for the first two years, which would mean they could stay in Louisville till I graduated from high school.

Mother's doctor at the University College Hospital had his doubts about the wisdom of this plan. Mother had gone to see him, she told Eleanor, because she had "been feeling so wretched—chest trouble, numb, headache." He found that there was nothing organically wrong but that she was in an extreme state of tension. He gave her pills he hoped would help. Hearing about the proposal that she take half a dozen more teenagers under her wing, he suggested that this could make her "condition," as she called it, worse. She, for her part, reasoned that her "condition" was partly due to the very thought of leaving me behind in the States to finish high school.

Running the MK house in Louisville for two years would mean she and Daddy could see me through high school.

Reading this letter years later, I had to pause to catch my breath. Did I ever have any idea that Mother had a "condition"? I knew that she often could not sleep—she would get up in the night and sit on our screened-in porch crocheting doilies to place under iced-tea glasses when we had company for dinner. But not until I read her letters did I see what a struggle she had staying afloat through her father's death that first year in the Gold Coast, then Billy's illnesses, then the avalanche of company and housekeeping in Ibadan on top of typing and editing and keeping books for the Training Union and teaching classes at the chapel and teaching me and Billy. Then I left for Newton when I was twelve, and now that I have my own daughter, I know how hard that must have been.

Nearing our journey home, she faced a much longer separation between us. After two years together in Louisville, she and Daddy would return to Nigeria for a new term, and then another and another for twenty more years. Her heart was breaking, she told Eleanor, as she packed up the things they were sending home for me. She let me decide what to take from my old life to the new—my desk, my grandmother's bed, which I would still have decades later. In years to come, my daughter would sleep in the little bed until it got too short for her. The desk would hold documents I wanted to be sure to keep: birth certificates, photos, a Lone Ranger comic. My parents kept my letters from Newton, tucked away in department store boxes tied up with string—waiting for me to read them and rediscover this family story, now nearly at its end.

A boy I liked was with us at the hostel in Lagos before we flew out of Nigeria on June 17, 1960, and for our farewell night together, he and I went down to the Lagos marina. As we left the hostel, one parent—his or mine—murmured a warning to behave. We sat side by side on a dock, our feet dangling. I wanted something dramatic to happen on my last night in West Africa. Nothing did. Lights twinkled on the canoes tied up along the shore. Voices murmured. The lagoon lay dark before us.

O Lost

And then it was over. Africa had vanished, except in memory and imagination. Anyone who has left her childhood home for good knows how odd that feels. Those early years anchored us to the earth. We found our footing in that world under those trees, in the shade of those houses, under that sky full of stars, with those people whose voices rose and fell in the way they did, whose bodies moved in their particular ways.

Transplanted to the United States, I faltered. I resented the time I wasted in high school classes where one teacher threw erasers at students who misbehaved and another went interminably on about the virtues of the John Birch Society. I hated walking from school to the bus stop in the grey cold of winter, my spirits so leaden that I wondered what was wrong with me. Despite the familiar presence of the other MKs who lived with us in Louisville, those two high school years were bleak, and then, in the fall of 1962, I was off to a North Carolina college where what I thought was solid ground kept crumbling under my feet. Girls in my dorm laughed at me because I didn't know rubbers were not just galoshes. A succession of boys left me spinning with confused desire. And where was that rock of faith to anchor me safe in this turbulent sea? I confessed in a journal entry that I was not sure I believed in God: "I don't feel anything— it looks like I'd know if he was there." For that matter, I wrote, "I don't remember ever really feeling the presence of God."

Accepting my unbelief, I quit going to church except when I visited family. In the years to come, I did attend a couple of Unitarian churches and tried warming myself by the Quakers' inner light, but however loosely I tried to define God, I was never able to make the leap of faith. I appreciate Henry Adams' testimony in *The Education of Henry Adams* that while as a boy "he prayed; he went through all the forms…neither to him nor to his brothers or sisters was religion real. Even the mild discipline of the Unitarian Church was so irksome that they all threw it off at the first possible moment, and never afterwards entered a church. The religious instinct had vanished, and could not be revived, although one made in later life many efforts to recover it." That has been my experience.

Hurled out of the small close mission community into a world of unpredictable American strangers, I felt like Ralph Ellison's Invisible Man when he went north and dropped through trapdoors with every step. His story spoke so directly to me that I took it as the subject of my master's thesis at the University of Louisville. "That's the way I feel," I explained to my adviser, the African-American poet Robert Hayden. "I don't feel at home in America." Perhaps feeling the same way himself, he reassured me: "You are a citizen of the world."

It was something, but not enough. After all those years of calling America "home" when I was in Africa, once I was actually in America I felt foreign, adrift between two continents, belonging to neither and physically separated from one. I would get whiffs of West Africa in letters from Mother and Daddy, and while I was in college, I went back to Nigeria the summer of 1964 with hopes for renewal. Instead, I felt a foreigner, distant from the people, their ways. I confessed what I felt to my friend Gita's mother one afternoon by the tennis court in Ogbomosho, and she said that even her husband, who spent nights in village huts and loved the Fulani people he worked with, did not really understand them. I appreciated her honesty, but what she said underlined the bleak truth of my childhood world: that this place and its people, the foundation of my life, alien to me in my grown-up years, had been alien all along.

As my life went on, my time in West Africa came to seem less important to who I was than all that happened later. Weary of the stereotypes that descended if I said I grew up in Africa and, yes, my parents were missionaries, I all but stopped mentioning my African past. I put it behind me. Over there was Africa. I was here now, in America. I hiked at Red River, where my Mother picked beans as a girl. I settled into a marriage a few blocks from where I had gone to grade school in Louisville. I got a Ph.D. in English literature and teaching jobs first at Maysville, Kentucky, then at Eastern Kentucky University, where my Mother had gone to college. I got a divorce. In 1977 I crossed the country alone, camping, seeing the great deserts and mountains of the American west, scenes I had first met in comics. I settled down in the San Francisco Bay area, teaching, writing, editing, hiking, canoeing, and finding in Oakland, with its sprays of bougainvillea and a sizable black population, what I had never before felt in America: a place of my heart.

I returned to West Africa again in 1979, when I was thirty-four. My parents were by this time directing mission work in Benin, a sliver of a country just west of Nigeria. They had spent a year in France in their fifties to learn French and seemed to enjoy their lives in this new place—the little church where Daddy preached in French, croissants and coffee at a beach hotel, friendship with church members and French expatriates. After a pleasant visit in their modern Cotonou house with its walled garden, we drove to Nigeria. It was a difficult homecoming. Nigeria had been shaken by the Biafran war and repeated coups. Oil had unleashed corruption. Highways were deadly. In Iwo, my beloved Rocks were gone from the earth—quarried away. The big old house in Oyo had been torn down. A concrete bungalow stood in its stead, surrounded by a field of corn. I was very nearly arrested for taking a photograph of a towering garbage heap in an Ibadan street. We cut our journey short and retreated to Benin, where even under a revolutionary military leader, I felt safer than I did in Nigeria, the country where I grew up.

Six years later I returned to Ghana, traveling with a photographer to report on how things were going there under Jerry Rawlings, the flight lieutenant who had taken power in a coup. Riding into Accra from the airport in the early morning, I had the impression I was passing through a war zone. Smoke hung over low buildings that looked, in that light, like ruins—

so unfamiliar had urban West Africa become to me. Over the next several weeks, I interviewed dissidents who had been imprisoned by Rawlings and talked to officials, labor leaders, market women.

We spent several days in Kumasi, which might have been a town I had never set foot in for all I remembered of it. There, a journalist whose newspaper had been critical of Rawlings helped me make contacts with people I wanted to interview. Peggy Appiah, the English wife of political leader Joseph Appiah, gave me a ride to town and later tea in her home. At a hilltop village to the North, a group of men invited me into a cave for a ceremony that they promised would produce for me a husband. A small chicken was sacrificed in the cause while I watched, sorry for the chicken and bemused by my own motivation for being there.

After the photographer and I separated so I could go south for interviews, he was arrested crossing into Burkina Faso without a visa and imprisoned there for several days. Ghanaians I had met in Accra rallied around me. Rawlings' own press assistant alerted Rawlings himself, and when Burkina Faso's head of state visited Accra, Rawlings told him, "You know that American photographer you have in prison? He has an appointment to take my picture. If you would let him go, he could do that," and he did.

Even in these uneasy times, Ghanaians across the political spectrum were going out of their way to help us, smooth our paths. As an adult moving in a West African adult world outside the American mission circle, I finally felt not so much a stranger. What would it be like, I wondered, to stay on

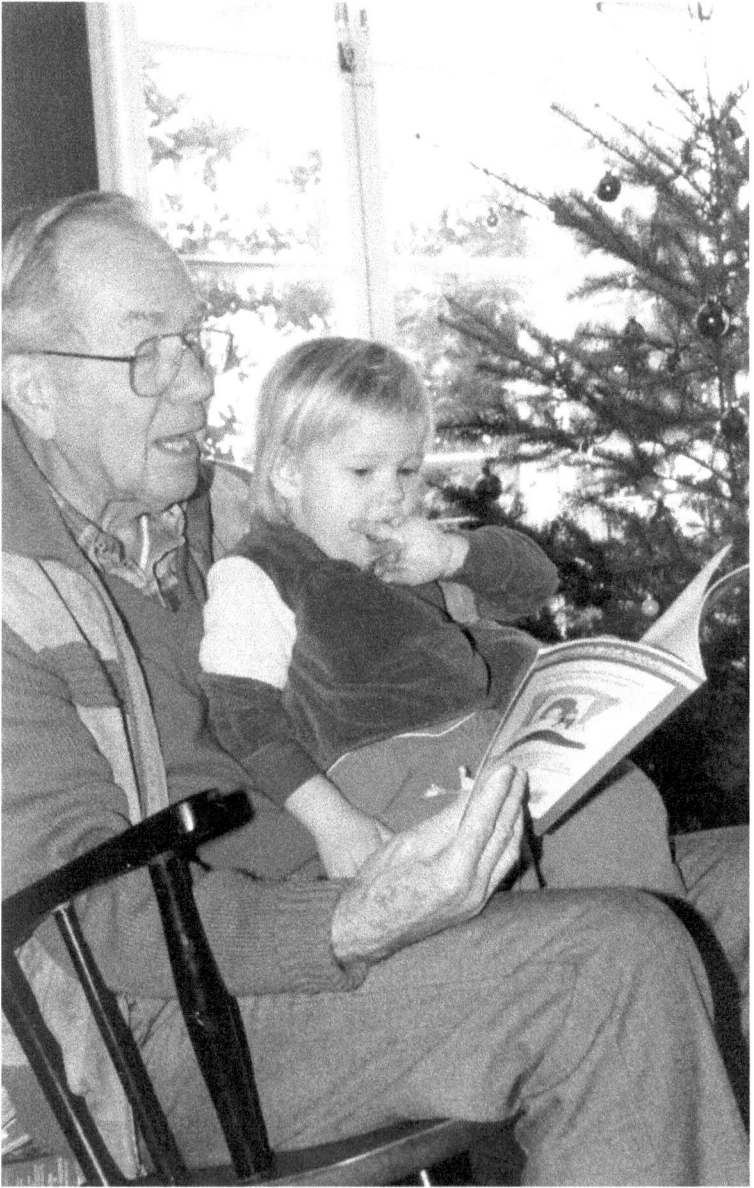

Daddy reading to my daughter, Cora

in Ghana—to live there, perhaps find that promised husband there? Wherever I was, I would always be in some way an expatriate, living life on the margins. Why not there?

In the end, I returned to California, where I surprised myself and shocked my parents by having a daughter on my own without the assurance of her father's presence. She turned out to be a gift for us all. For years I had not seen much of my parents, who in retirement had settled in Lawrenceburg, Kentucky, with winter stints to Florida, where they put their French to use in a Haitian congregation. For a long time my withdrawal from the Baptist faith stood between us, especially between my father and me, though I went to church when I visited them and once took them to a Unitarian church when they came to see me in Oakland. Daddy observed that throughout the service he had not heard a mention of Jesus Christ. However pleasant our visits to one another, a chill hung in the air.

The birth of my daughter, Cora, changed that. Things might have gone another way—it was not easy for my parents, especially my mother, child of the early twentieth century, to see me become an unwed mother. When I was several months pregnant, my brother, himself married, invited us all to Aiken, South Carolina, where he taught at a University of South Carolina campus. Through Bill's intervention, my parents and I made our peace. The years to come were, in the language of my former faith, a redemptive time.

For the first three years of Cora's life, Mother and Daddy trekked out from Kentucky to California to help take care of her while I went back to work, and when I took a teaching job at Indiana University in Bloomington in 1989, they moved into

Mother and Daddy in the Winchester church where
they were married half a century earlier

a retirement center across town to be near us. Getting to know my parents differently once they were no longer missionaries, I found myself surprised by how much they could enjoy life, given time. They chatted in the dining room with residents who, like themselves, were well traveled. They spoke French over dinner at the French table once a week. Daddy took up pool, which he introduced to his three granddaughters when Bill, his wife, Sandy, and daughters Lauren and Megan came to visit.

Battered by his early years of illness and medication, Bill had had his own lonely struggles adjusting to American life, remembering that even in fifth grade in the United States he had felt his *otherness* as he walked down the school halls. From time to time he and I talked about other differences that growing up in West Africa had made to our lives. Neither one of us had managed to become the fiction writers we had hoped we might be, and we wondered if that was because our cultural foundation was not firm—we could not write as either Africans or Americans, or even as immigrants from one place to another. Like moths to a flame we were drawn to African and African-American writers: I as a writer of history, Bill as a teacher of literature. Yet like me, Bill did not talk often about his African experience, even in his classes—because, as he told students once, he now knew too much of the damage the West had done to Africa. One of his African-American students spoke a healing word we could both take to heart. Don't hide your experience, the student said: *Celebrate* it.

Despite our mission past, neither one of us had remained more than very occasional churchgoers, although when Bill and his family visited we all went together to my parents' small University Baptist Church, where the minister was a woman. When the Baptist association voted on whether to expel the church for letting a woman lead it, Daddy told those assembled that he had worked side by side with women on the mission field, and he knew they could do any church work as well as men. His counsel did not prevail and his heart failed not long after that, in 1998, when he was eighty-three.

My mother lived ten more years without him—a hard, hard time for her at first, becoming easier in some ways as she let loose of the burden of responsibilities she had carried for so long. As she neared death at the age of ninety-six, she and I spent a gentle hour remembering her life—naming, one by one, people who had been important to her. Among them was Enid Whirley, who had called her from time to time from her home in Alabama. Sitting on the side of her bed, Mother looked straight at me and said, "We've known each other for a long time, haven't we?" In that twilight moment, I believed that she thought I was Enid, and I felt the affection between them.

With Mother's death, my closest link to my childhood in Africa was broken. In all these years, I had made little effort to stay in touch with other missionary kids. Nor did I attend the annual Nigerian mission reunion in Alabama, although after my brother started a Nigerian MK Facebook page, I read and posted on it, fascinated by how much it meant to see our childhood world float to the surface. Bit by bit we reconstituted our distant past: particular trees on particular compounds, the blocks we built houses with at the Lagos

*Visiting the cemetery in Mt. Sterling, Kentucky, where
Mother's father and mother were buried: Daddy, Cora,
Mother, Megan, Lauren, Sandy, and Bill*

After Daddy's death: at Cora's and my house in Bloomington, Indiana

hostel, the missionary "aunts" and "uncles" whose faces we scanned from old mission yearbooks.

After I retired and moved to North Carolina to be nearer my daughter (who followed family tradition and became a teacher), Gita Richardson Larson and I renewed our sisterhood in what is now our town, Asheville. Michael Taylor joined us for dinner when his work brought him our way, and others from our Nigerian days dropped by from time to time: John Whirley, his brother, Philip, Elaine Neil Orr, and in an unforgettable evening, Roger, Richard, and Robert Congdon: still recognizably the boys I climbed the rocks with all those years ago. A world I had lost began to come reassuringly again to view, and I saw more clearly how present it had been all along: in the odd-angled view from which I see American life, in my delight at finding my feet on a worn dirt path in a concrete city.

I took to traveling to Costa Rica where I could feel at home amid the bougainvillea and mango trees, the dirt roads of country towns, and a language not my own. At a San Jose hostel one morning I struck up a conversation with a man staring stonily at television in the lounge. He had just arrived two days before in Costa Rica. "There is much trouble in my country," he explained.

"What country is that?" I asked, already knowing the answer.

"Nigeria," he said.

"It is mine, too," I replied. I told him my story, briefly, and he told me his, so bleak that when it was done I hardly knew what to say. He was a Christian Yoruba living in Jos when his wife and child were killed in an upheaval I had read about in the news. He had fled the country, making his way across West Africa and then taking a ship that landed in Costa Rica, where the government gave him refugee status and put him up in the hostel where he awaited guidance in this country that spoke a language he knew not one word of. He seemed a man stunned, immobilized by what life had handed him.

I looked for a question that would not open up a Pandora's box of grief. I asked him what work he had done in Nigeria. He had been an artist—making cloth prints. I had three hours left before I was to leave for the airport. We could walk together to the Museum of Costa Rican Art, I said. It was not far. Would he like that?

Yes, he said. Yes.

Together we strolled through the park to the white stucco building that had once been an airport terminal. I had seen the exhibits before but now saw them differently as he, with his artist's eye, pointed out this or that thing I had missed. He reached up to touch a piece. He stood amazed before one large dark installation of a damaged world. The museum visit lifted his spirits a little, I thought, and on the way back to the hostel he spoke of his determination to survive and make a new life, and I believed that he would. Before we parted, I gave him my Spanish dictionary; he gave me a brotherly kiss on the cheek—two Nigerians, meeting for a morning in a town far from home.

Friday, Oct. 8, 1948

282nd day — 84 days follow

Up at 6:30 - Slept like a log. After breakfast, began copying Eng. II. articles. Copied one - C.A. had patch + needed rest from books - So I pushed her swing a bit. Then copied other article. Noon caught me. Afterward, typed part of article - rocked C.A. to sleep, rested very briefly. Then finished typing the lesson. Emma copied last one. (She did 3) I was ready at language time to mail them, I went on & Rev. Down taught Emma, Back, we studied 4 pages (new). Finished we showed him Christmas play. He liked it. Dinner was ready 5:10. Raphael needs more work. Too early dinner. Afterward, we played badminton — Mr. Brad had asked Emma to see his flowers. She did — (we). Rain came - We had to stop. C.A. & I played dominoes. She does real well. I wrote Mother. — Diary - Read Bible - I am so tired. I must go to bed.

This has been a good day but a hard day. So much wgt. off my shoulders even though not too pleased about the work-manship. Goodnight —

Tomorrow is coming.

Entry in my father's 1948-49 journal, now in the Lilly Library, Indiana University

Acknowledgments

A fter my father's death, my mother put our family letters from these African years in chronological order and donated them to the Lilly Library at Indiana University, Bloomington. These letters, rich in the details of our daily life, were a significant resource for me as I wrote this story of our lives in West Africa. The Lilly archived the personal letters as the Claxon mss. (685 items); a later set of documents became the Claxon mss. II (5,000 items). Descriptions of both collections are available on the Lilly Library website.

My brother and I are grateful to Lilly manuscripts curators Saundra Taylor and Cherry Williams for understanding what these papers contribute to the history of missions and of life in West Africa during this period. We thank, too, the various staff members who have worked to make the papers accessible, not only to scholars but, as is the Lilly's admirable policy, to anyone who may wish to look at them.

Most of the photographs in this book are from family albums or slides. Wilfred Congdon's Newton photographs are published by permission of Roger Congdon; my thanks to Robert Congdon for providing scans of these slides and Roger for providing scans of photos in his possession. The photo of Newton orchestra practice is used by permission of Charles L. Gillespie, International Mission Board, Southern Baptist

Convention. I acquired the War Office maps of the Gold Coast and Nigeria from a collector in the United Kingdom, David Druett of Pennymead Books, who kindly saw that they arrived expeditiously and in good condition.

For responding to my questions about the Yoruba language, practices, and traditions, I thank Akintunde Akinyemi of the University of Florida and Akin Adesokan of Indiana University. Jon Kay, director of Traditional Arts Indiana, spent several hours showing me how to discover cultural dimensions of family photographs. His guidance proved helpful when I selected photographs for the book. I spent several early weeks working on the book at Hambidge Center in Rabun Gap, Georgia, and I appreciate that writing time and the fellowship around the dinner table.

For commenting on the manuscript I thank my brother, Bill Claxon; my daughter, Cora Polsgrove, and friends Gerald Coomer, Clifton Hawkins, George Ella Lyon, Peggy McCurdy, Radhika Parameswaran, Rick Ryan, Carol Sklenicka, and Isabelle White. For offering counsel at various stages, I thank Becky O'Malley, Carolyn Oppenheim, Carol Stangler. I thank Gita Richardson Larson for our many discussions of our MK lives and my friend Holly Stocking for helping me see what I owe to my African childhood.

Finally, I appreciate the grace with which Mikesch Muecke, guiding light of Culicidae Press, turned my ideas about interweaving text and pictures into the reality of this book.

www.ingramcontent.com/pod-product-compliance
Lightning Source LLC
Chambersburg PA
CBHW052005090426
42741CB00008B/1563